NEW MODERNIST TYPE

NEW
MODERN

STEVEN HELLER
GAIL ANDERSON

Thames & Hudson

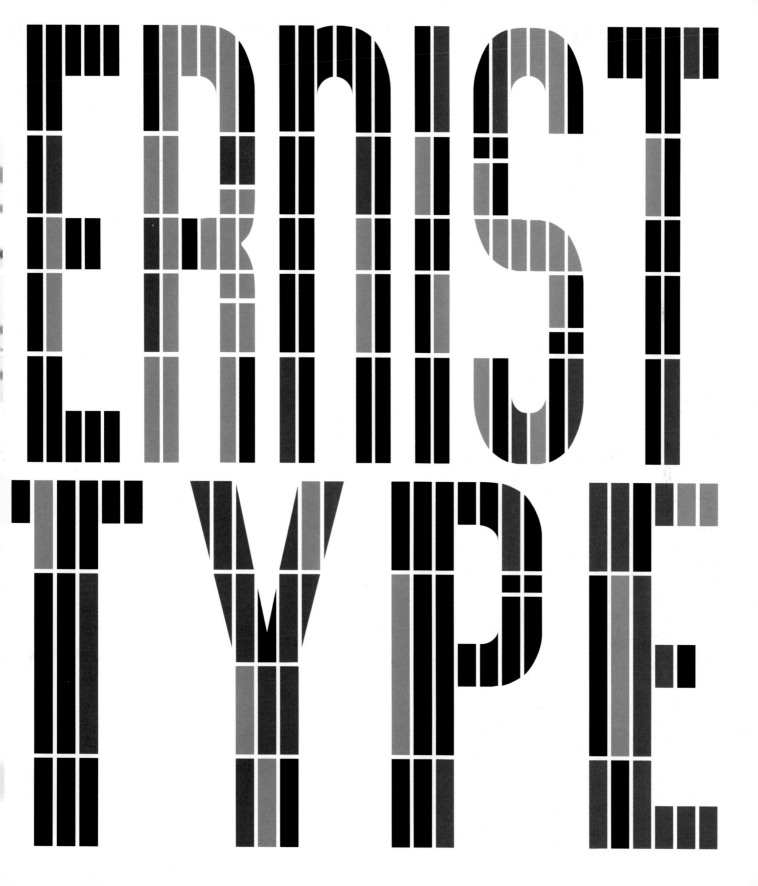

For Louise Fili & Nicolas Heller – S. H.

For Lloyd & Nola Anderson – G. A.

First published in 2012 in hardcover in the United States of America by Thames & Hudson Inc., 500 Fifth Avenue, New York, New York 10110

thamesandhudsonusa.com

Library of Congress Catalog Card Number 2011946036

ISBN 978-0-500-24141-7

Printed and bound in China by Everbest Printing Co. Ltd

4

ACKNOWLEDGMENTS

It's a trifecta! *New Vintage Type*, *New Ornamental Type*, and, finally, *New Modernist Type*. We'd like to thank our friends at Thames & Hudson, who made the series possible and put up with many *Modernist* e-mails, one office visit, and lots of questions on both the e-mails and the visit. Their guidance and support has been invaluable, as always.

We couldn't have got this one done without intrepid research assistance from our old pal, Christine Thompson Maichin, and our new pal, Abigail Steinem (the most cheerful young designer ever). Christine gave birth to Jaclyn during *New Vintage*, and then to Robert during *New Ornamental*, but was apparently unwilling to give us a *Modernist* baby to add to the set.

Gratitude is also extended to Portia Hubert for pitching in when we were swamped and to talented type designer Bonnie Clas for our handsome modern typeface, Mecano Neue.

On to the next book!

DESIGN
Gail Anderson
Abigail Steinem

RESEARCH
Christine Thompson Maichin
Abigail Steinem

Mecano Neue typeface
by Bonnie Clas
(based on Fregio Mecano)

– S. H. & G. A.

INTRODUCTION

It means integrity; it means honesty; it means the absence of sentimentality and the absence of nostalgia; it means simplicity; it means clarity. That's what modernism means to me.

—PAUL RAND, 1996

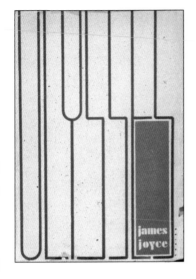

ULYSSES • Book cover by Ernst Reichl, 1934. This unusual typographic design eschews conventional illustration for demonstrative yet economically modernist lettering.

IF PAUL RAND'S DEFINITION had been the driving force behind *New Modernist Type*, there might not be a book. For while the work contained in these pages, all of it produced since the turn of the 21st century, has integrity, honesty, simplicity, and clarity, the presence of sentimentality and nostalgia is unavoidable – and actually welcome. This is not a treacly or kitsch-y nostalgia but an homage to the styles and methods of the past that have resonance today. Despite postmodernism and all the reactionary, eclectic approaches it comprises, modernism never entirely disappeared. Nonetheless, the classic and orthodox modernisms of the 1920s through to the 1960s – from the Bauhaus to the International Style – did become either oppressively rigid or excessively conservative, triggering rejection and rebellion.

In art, design, and fashion, it usually requires one or two generations to reappreciate the virtues of who and what came before. By the mid-1950s, modern graphic design had settled into a familiar universal language used by businesses and governments, bringing the tipping point for wholesale rejection by young designers. In the 1980s and 1990s, a veritable culture clash between moderns and postmoderns (including Deconstruction, New Wave, Grunge, Neo-Dada, and Punk) was in full tilt, and young designers threw Helvetica and the baby out with the bathwater. Once this purging was exhausted, it was propitious to reintroduce modernist type and other kindred formulas back into the toolkit.

A new take on old modern took hold with Neville Brody's work for *The Face* magazine – including a renewed passion for Helvetica – and *Wallpaper** later reintroduced a post-postmodern clarity and cleanliness to its lifestyle format. Perhaps as a rejection of the digital-grunge clutter and anarchy triggered by David Carson's *Ray Gun* and its adherents, readability, legibility, and simplicity invariably returned. And as the 2000s rolled around, these fundamental design tenets reappeared with a vengeance.

And yet this return to a modernist aesthetic represented only a portion of what must be viewed as the age of typographic eclecticism-run-rampant. So many passé styles and retrograde forms were coming back into fashion, it made the hard disk spin. This old-becomes-new phenomenon manifested itself in altered and nuanced ways; it prompted us to take a new look at how the old became new – again.

Hence a series of three books. First we published *New Vintage Type*, a collection of historical homage to and pastiche of classic fonts. Then came *New Ornamental Type*, the revival of a pre-modern decorative aesthetic that involved retro, proto, and contemporary ornamental typographic applications. Now, here is *New Modernist Type*, which, curiously enough, also includes a fair share of vintage alphabets (or "alphabetics" as we call the playful nuances exhibited here) but implies the revival of modernist simplicity with a timeless, veritably style-less sensibility.

The word "modern" is a noun, an adjective, and the root of a verb ("modernize"). It is a period of time and a stylistic representation of that time. It is an aesthetic approach and a philosophical mandate. Modern is the defining design current of the 20th century. There is classic modern, mid-century modern, and postmodern. The first two are inspirationally related while postmodern is a rejection of that relationship. Classic modern is the radical overthrow of antiquated governing design principles, such as central-axis composition, ornamental excesses, and archaic typographies. It is the establishment of new standards of rightness – and wrongness – and the introduction of a new formal language rooted in geometry, simplicity, and functionality. In the words of Jan Tschichold, one of its foremost graphic design pioneers, classic modern is "elementary," without flourish. Mid-century modern was the propagation of the tenets of classic modern throughout the world of mass production and consumption.

Helvetica and Univers are the emblems of mid-century modern's typographic language, but other typefaces are also part of the legacy of unadorned typographic neutrality. For example, Akzidenz and other bold sans serifs were used during the 1950s and 1960s as a means of universalizing graphic messages. The Swiss and the International schools and styles of design and typography carried the torch of clarity, while 1950s magazines like *Neue Grafik* showed how orthodox or pure modern typography could level the communications playing field.

Mid-century modern designers became fanatical about what they believed was "the rightness of form." Rigidity was the objective of modern practice. For some it was an ideology, for others it was a religion, and for others still it was both. Modernism was the answer to the world's woes. And yet, in turning into this false panacea it also triggered rebellion.

Although the most dedicated of the moderns, among them Paul Rand, Alvin Lustig, Lester Beall, Rudolph de Harak, and Ivan Chermayeff, did not abandon their distinct visual personalities – they just limited the number of colors and typefaces – modernism was perceived by many non-believers as a limited set of strictly enforced principles. In fact, the grid, which was simply an organizational tool, was viewed by the more innately eclectic as a prison gate.

Granted, the most radical members of the International School were extremely parochial, but within those modernist constraints there existed countless ways to bust the grid and create individual work.

One paradox of mid-century modern is that it was at once a flowering of innovation and a hardening of modernist rules. For every individual there were scores of designers who rigidly followed modern tenets – some of them did not even know their work was modern, but rather accepted it as the way typography was done. As a result, modernism was seen by many younger designers as something to be avoided – like buzzcut haircuts in the hippy days.

What these fashion-conscious rebels did not entirely understand was that modernism was not as strict as it was made out to be. Rand's definition (opposite) was rather open to interpretation. What's more, the goals of modern typography were never as one-dimensional as they seemed. Even Rand emphatically stated: "Simplicity is not the goal; it is the by-product of a good idea and modest expectations."

For those who saw modern type as only Helvetica, and modern design as only Swiss, Rand said: "When I was first aware of what the Swiss were doing, I used to ridicule it. I really felt the stuff was cold, and all the other clichés people use to describe Swiss design. But then I changed completely.... Granted that there is a lot of lousy, very stiff, and very cold stuff. But there is no counterpart to Swiss design in terms of something that you can describe, that you can follow, that you can systematically understand. It just makes sense."

Some designers who returned to modern typography in the late 2000s did so because it felt and looked good in comparison with more cluttered design. Others followed Rand's route. Analytically speaking, working with a limited type and color palette does not hamper expression or hinder distinction. Making readability paramount does not necessarily exclude complexity.

The definition of modernist typography has changed with time, albeit in a minor way. As Rand wrote in *Good Design Is Good Will* (1987), "The difference between modern and traditional typography is not the difference between apples and oranges. It is more like the difference between Granny Smith and Golden Delicious."

A collection of examples showing how simplicity and homage to historical modernism have impacted contemporary graphic design, *New Modernist Type* is a rich sourcebook of ideas for the most functional of styles.

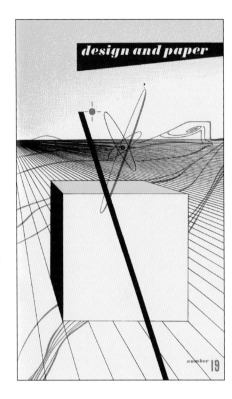

DESIGN AND PAPER #19 • Marquardt and Co., mini-portfolio, 1945. Designed by Ladislav Sutnar, a Czech Constructivist who introduced modern methods of presenting data through information graphics.

1990 CUMMINS ENGINE ANNUAL REPORT • Designed by Paul Rand, who combined playful and functional design into a signature mid-century modernist approach.

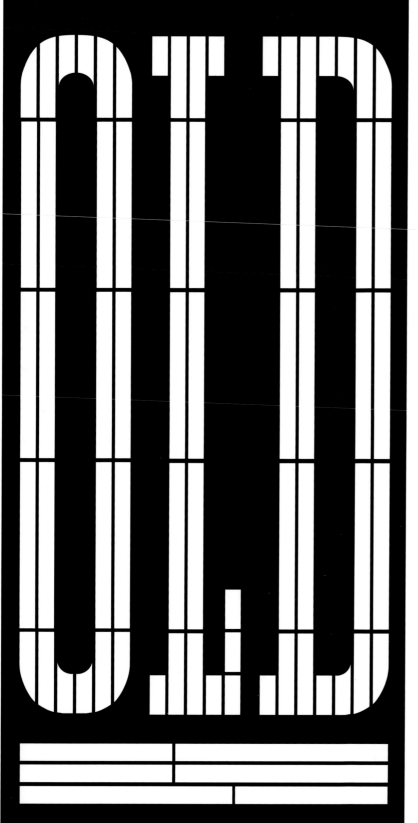

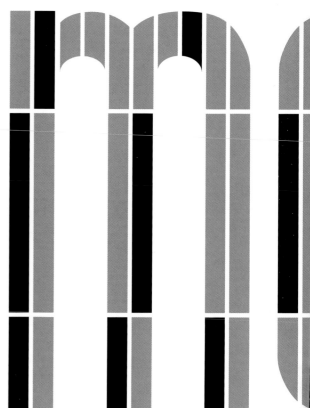

"OLD" AND "MODERN" are not opposing terms. The first documented usage of the word "modern" dates back to the late 16th century; it meant "of present or recent times" and was contrasted with "ancient." The here and now versus the there and then – that was modern. The Latin *modernus*, "modern," was derived from the Latin *modo*, meaning "just now." And so "modern" is defined as specifically "what pertained to present times and to what was new and not old-fashioned."

By the 19th and 20th centuries, Modern (with a capital M) was used to designate movements in art, and modernism developed into various different groups and offshoots.

When viewed as a movement or manifestation, the word "modern" invariably becomes locked in time. Schools, trends, and styles usually have finite existences. There is always a newer or a more reactionary entity that will vie for ascendancy and superiority. Although art nouveau was considered modern in the 1890s, it was generally deemed passé after the turn

of the 20th century. How could a current of art and design so revolutionary become, in just a decade or so, un-modern?

It is the indisputable nature of style to slide in and out of, well, style, but the notion of what is "modern" is also the result of cultural standards. Between the golden age of art nouveau (which developed into the *Modernista* movement in Spain) and the early 20th century the Western world shifted technologically, politically, and socially, and so did the look and content of that era's art and design.

When modernists cut the serpentine tendrils off art nouveau objects and replaced curvilinear forms with right angles, they altered the landscape and the language of virtually everything in the design world, from architecture to typefaces. They believed that this would be the ultimate change, the revolution to end all revolutions.

But, even within modernism, differences in style, form, and philosophy prevailed. The Futurists were different from the Constructivists; and while the Bauhaus borrowed certain tenets from De Stijl, each group embraced variegated nuances.

When modernism began to morph from Expressionism to Rationalism, or from Vorticism to Surrealism, elements of the modernist creed changed. There were many splintered modernisms – some inextricably wedded to the moment, others ostensibly timeless. Old modern was anything that happened to have fallen from grace. Rejected by Stalin, Constructivism disappeared. Rejected by Hitler, the Bauhaus closed shop. With the decline of these movements, modernist styles lost their freshness.

The examples in this section draw directly from the aspects of modernism that were once iconic before becoming old-fashioned. Some of these styles and methods were resurrected because they were indeed still functional; others were revived as pastiche, kitsch, or (to be generous) for the joy and beauty of the forms.

FUNCTIONAL

This is perhaps the most specific catch-all category yet. Modernism was about functional design –
clear and clean communication, exemplified by equally crisp line and shape. In recent years, following
a 1990s trend for anarchic typography, functionality has returned – but often in surprising ways.

WHAT ARE YOU REALLY WORTH • What better way
to introduce a special issue about money than a metallic
gold background and a bold query? "The scale and
simplicity of the cover line treatment," says Bichler,
"counteract the complex nature of financial statistics
and set the tone for a piece that dared Americans to
evaluate their financial well-being." **DESIGN FIRM:** *The
New York Times Magazine* **DESIGN DIRECTOR:** Arem
Duplessis **ART DIRECTOR:** Gail Bichler **DESIGNER:** Hilary
Greenbaum **CLIENT:** *The New York Times* **PRIMARY
FONTS:** Theinhardt, Knockout

SECURITY • Part thriller, part social satire, this is the story
of a crime that lies hidden behind the trappings of suburban
security. The design was influenced by "the neighborhood watch
sign from my childhood suburb and a little bit of Paul Rand [the
eye]," says Jennifer Carrow. **ART DIRECTOR:** Susan Mitchell
DESIGNER: Jennifer Carrow **CLIENT:** Farrar, Straus and Giroux
PRIMARY FONT: Akzidenz-Grotesk

THE REDBREAST • To "freshen the thriller-novel look" with this hardcover redesign, Adam Johnson was influenced (although not overtly) by Saul Bass's 1950s and 1960s movie posters. **DESIGN FIRM:** HarperCollins **ART DIRECTORS:** Robin Bilardello, Milan Bozic **DESIGNER AND ILLUSTRATOR:** Adam Johnson **PHOTOGRAPHER:** John Livze/Getty Images **CLIENT:** Harper Paperbacks **PRIMARY FONT:** Knockout

DISKO ESPERANTO • This poster was designed for a monthly event about global music, "so I transformed a globe and a disk into 'Disko Esperanto'," says Götz Gramlich. The basis for the typography is Russian Constructivism and what the designer calls "reduced Swiss." **DESIGN FIRM:** gggrafik **ART DIRECTOR, DESIGNER, AND ILLUSTRATOR:** Götz Gramlich **CLIENT:** Alte Feuerwache Mannheim **PRIMARY FONT:** Gravur Condensed

FUNCTIONAL

21ST-CENTURY MOTHERHOOD • "I wanted to juxtapose a very idyllic Victorian image of motherhood with a modern, digital typeface: OCR-A," says Catherine Casalino, whose monochromatic design subtly addresses the subject. **DESIGN FIRM:** Catherine Casalino Design **ART DIRECTOR:** Julia Kushnirsky **DESIGNER:** Catherine Casalino **PHOTOGRAPHER:** RF Image **CLIENT AND PUBLISHER:** Columbia University Press **PRIMARY FONT:** OCR-A

WAKE UP • 1950s pulp novels "loosely influenced" Jack Kerouac's biography of the Buddha. "Because of the weight which Kerouac's name carries and the great title of the book, it was best to make them both as big as possible," Gregg Kulick says. "I made the cover extremely simple typographically but I put everything on a slant to show the immediacy of the title. Then, I placed a traditional Buddhist pattern reconstructed from the door of a Buddhist monastery over everything." **DESIGN FIRM:** Penguin Design Department **ART DIRECTOR:** Paul Buckley **DESIGNER:** Gregg Kulick **CLIENT:** Penguin Books **PRIMARY FONT:** Trade Gothic

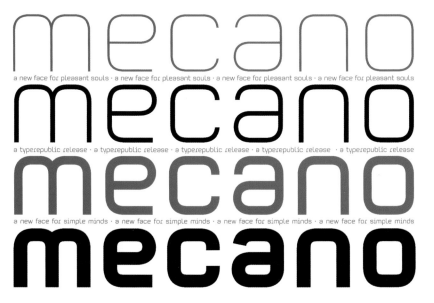

MECANO TYPEFACE • This typeface is based on geometric structures. The shapes are wide open and simple, which reflects the spirit of mechanical technology.
DESIGN FIRM: Andreu Balius **DESIGNER:** Andreu Balius **CLIENT:** TypeRepublic
PRIMARY FONT: Mecano

KNOLL LUMIERE PAINT • In this student project, the challenge was to design an imaginary architectural paint line for an existing brand. Having chosen Knoll, Kristin Agnarsdóttir's influences were Knoll's iconic branding, Massimo Vignelli, Herbert Matter, and vintage Knoll catalogs. **DESIGN FIRM:** Dóttir **ART DIRECTOR AND DESIGNER:** Kristin Agnarsdóttir **CLIENT:** Student work **PRIMARY FONT:** Helvetica Neue

FUNCTIONAL

PAKISTAN • The decision to run this cover story on Pakistan in the 5 April 2009 issue came quite close to deadline. In the absence of imagery that represented the content, the designers "decided to go with a bold, somewhat retro, typographic approach." **DESIGN FIRM:** *The New York Times Magazine* **DESIGN DIRECTOR:** Arem Duplessis **ART DIRECTOR:** Gail Bichler **CLIENT:** *The New York Times* **PRIMARY FONTS:** Knockout, Sunday, Stymie

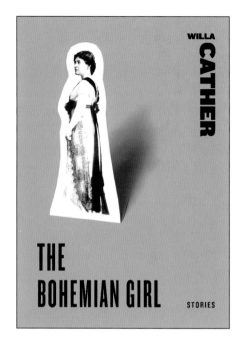

WILLA **CATHER**

THE
BOHEMIAN GIRL
STORIES

LEO **TOLSTOY**

FAMILY
HAPPINESS
STORIES

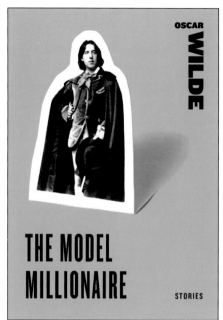

OSCAR **WILDE**

THE MODEL
MILLIONAIRE
STORIES

HERMAN **MELVILLE**

THE
HAPPY FAILURE
STORIES

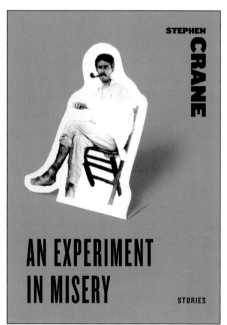

STEPHEN **CRANE**

AN EXPERIMENT
IN MISERY
STORIES

FYODOR **DOSTOYEVSKY**

A DISGRACEFUL
AFFAIR
STORIES

CLASSIC SHORTS • This redesigned short-story collection is geared towards a young audience. The design for the series was influenced by 1950s Swiss posters, big idea advertisements, and book covers. **ART DIRECTOR:** Robin Bilardello **DESIGNER:** Adam Johnson **PHOTOGRAPHER:** Benjamin Hill **CLIENT:** Harper Perennial **PRIMARY FONT:** Knockout

FUNCTIONAL

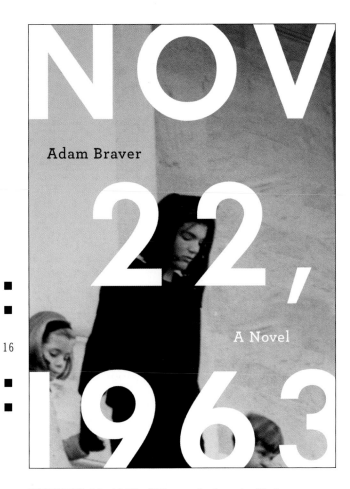

Adam Braver

NOV 22, 1963

A Novel

NOVEMBER 22, 1963 • With a captivating mix of fact and fiction, *November 22, 1963* chronicles the events surrounding JFK's assassination through the eyes of those closest to him on that day. The cover is a stark reminder of this tragic event. **ART DIRECTOR:** Rodrigo Corral **DESIGNER:** Christopher Brand **PHOTOGRAPHER:** Abbie Rowe, White House/John F. Kennedy Presidential Library, Boston **CLIENT:** Tin House **PRIMARY FONTS:** Futura, Archer

DÉLIVRÉ • The typeface Archer combines the ordinariness of antiques with the modern practicality of geometry. The purpose was to mix classical and literary references with a modern touch. **DESIGN FIRM:** Neutre **ART DIRECTOR AND DESIGNER:** Manu Blondiau **PHOTOGRAPHER:** Alain Géronnez **CLIENTS:** Rossi Contemporary, Évasions **PRIMARY FONT:** Archer

délivré

ART CONTEMPORAIN
EN BOUQUINERIE
HEDENDAAGSE KUNST
TUSSEN DE BOEKEN

11 artistes
pour un an
chez
Évasions 2

9 m²

Elke maand een kunstenaar bij Évasions 2

PROGRAMME ANNUEL / JAARLIJKS PROGRAMMA 2010-2011

OCTOBRE 2010 OKTOBER
Lionel Vinche
Sur l'art même

NOVEMBRE 2010 NOVEMBER
Guy Giraud
Tout lieu est un monde

DÉCEMBRE 2010 DECEMBER
Thomas
Mazzarella
Peintures

JANVIER 2011 JANUARI
Alain géronneZ
Main libre

FÉVRIER 2011 FEBRUARI
Luc Deleu
Espace orbain

MARS 2011 MAART
Xavier Martin
Sans titre

AVRIL 2011 APRIL
Anne De Gelas
La vie est un roman

MAI 2011 MEI
Carine Revael
Ouvrage

JUIN 2011 JUNI
Éric van Hove
Uqbar

JUILLET/AOÛT 2011 JULI/AUGUSTUS
Pierre-Étienne
Donnet
Extraits

SEPTEMBRE 2011 SEPTEMBER
Éléonore Gaillet
Trazabilidad

Évasions 2
rue du Midi 147 Zuidstraat . Bruxelles 1000 Brussel
T. 02 513 63 84 . **ouvert 365/365 open**
10:00 - 19:00 (dim./zon. 12:00 - 19:00)

En collaboration avec
In samenwerking met

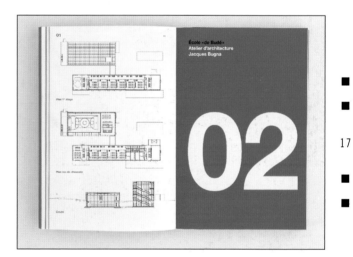

SIA 55 • This guide contains a selection of fifty-five recent and innovative architecture projects from Geneva. The inspiration here is obvious: classic Swiss graphic design. **DESIGN FIRM:** GVA Studio **CLIENT:** SIA (Société Suisse des Ingénieurs et des Architectes) **PRIMARY FONT:** Helvetica

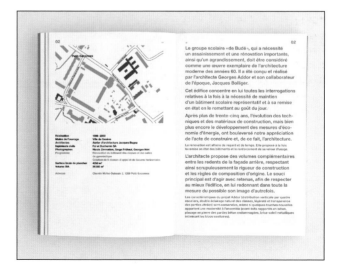

FUNCTIONAL

MORSE CODE • Henry's Drive wines are all branded along a postal theme. The Morse code range pays homage to the first electronic mail system. The varietal of each wine is printed on the label in Morse code. **DESIGN FIRM:** Parallax Design **DESIGNER:** Kellie Campbell-Illingworth **CLIENT:** Henry's Drive Vignerons **PRIMARY FONT:** Avenir

THE FEMALE THING • "The figures of Adam and Eve influenced this reassessment of feminism and women's ambivalence toward it," explains Archie Ferguson. **DESIGN FIRM:** Archie Ferguson Design **ART DIRECTOR AND DESIGNER:** Archie Ferguson **PHOTOGRAPHER:** Charles Gullung/Getty Images **CLIENT:** Pantheon Books **PRIMARY FONT:** Akzidenz-Grotesk

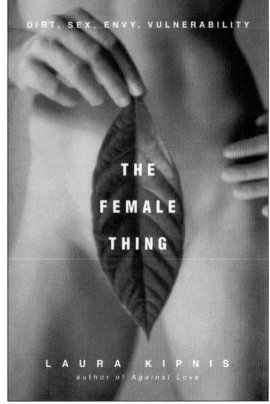

Nø.6 Cinema   issue **3**

Nø.6 Cinema   issue **5**

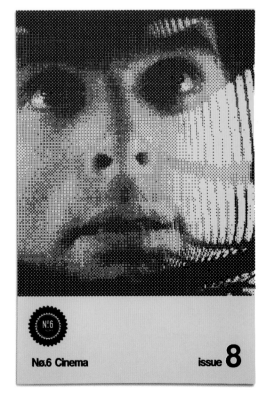

Nø.6 Cinema   issue **7**

Nø.6 Cinema   issue **8**

NO. 6 CINEMA LEAFLETS
• In this film listings leaflet designed for an independent cinema based in Portsmouth, the use of a modernist typeface reflects the contemporary style of the auditorium and the aesthetic of the arthouse films that are screened there daily. **DESIGN FIRM:** ilovedust **CLIENT:** No. 6 Cinema **PRIMARY FONT:** Helvetica Neue

FUNCTIONAL

ANTWERPEN LONKT • This is a suggestive book cover design for a collection of cultural and touristic posters (1940–2005) from the Letterenhuis's collection. **DESIGN FIRM:** Jan en Randoald **ART DIRECTORS:** Jan W. Hespeel, Randoald Sabbe **DESIGNERS:** Jan W. Hespeel, Randoald Sabbe **CLIENT:** City of Antwerp **PRIMARY FONT:** Futura Heavy

AN ETHICS OF INTERROGATION • A simple yet eerie cover for a book about the ethical, moral, and legal implications of interrogation and torture. **DESIGN FIRM:** The University of Chicago Press **ART DIRECTOR:** Jill Shimabukuro **DESIGNER:** Isaac Tobin **CLIENT:** The University of Chicago Press **PRIMARY FONTS:** Futura, Futura Bold

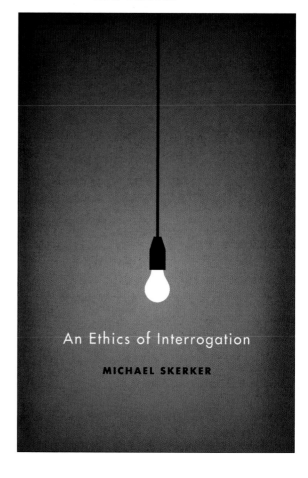

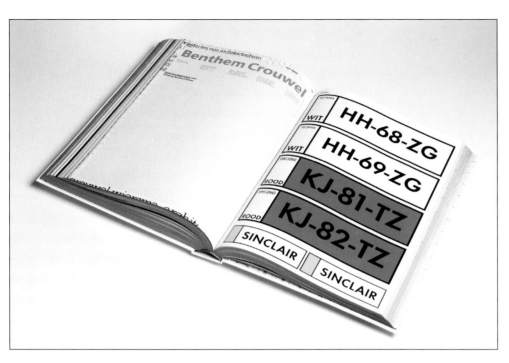

BC AD • "Our work is mostly influenced by modernist ideas and we are always aware that we are rooted in a long tradition of history of design," notes Dirk Laucke. "We never point to a single person or design item, because we always try to avoid creating vintage design or plagiarism." **DESIGN FIRM:** Studio Laucke Siebein **ART DIRECTORS AND DESIGNERS:** Dirk Laucke, Johanna Siebein **CLIENT:** Benthem Crouwel Architects **PRIMARY FONTS:** Akzidenz-Grotesk, Futura

DDC ROAD CREW, RULE NO. 01 • "I take wild road trips a couple of times a year," says Aaron Draplin, "and in 2007 I managed to stay out for a couple of months, all over the States. That's the spirit of this piece. There are ups and downs on the road, and you leave them out there!" **DESIGN FIRM:** Draplin Design Co. **ART DIRECTOR, DESIGNER, AND PHOTOGRAPHER:** Aaron James Draplin **CLIENT:** Draplin Design Co., Open Road Div. **PUBLISHER:** Draplin.com **PRIMARY FONTS:** Gardner, Futura Bold

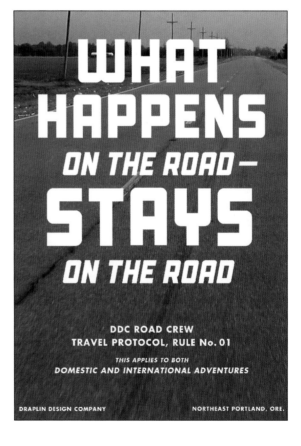

FUNCTIONAL

I AM A STRANGE LOOP by DOUGLAS HOFSTATDER

I AM A STRANGE LOOP • The typography of this book jacket, which Timothy Hsu says was influenced by Bauhaus, incorporates Swiss minimalism and artless functionality. **DESIGN FIRM:** Hsu + Associates **ART DIRECTORS:** Rick Pracher, Timothy Hsu **DESIGNER:** Timothy Hsu **ILLUSTRATOR:** Timothy Hsu **CLIENT:** Basic Books **PRIMARY FONT:** Trade Gothic

U.S. GREEN BUILDING COUNCIL • This design work aimed to convey the mission of the U.S. Green Building Council. "We created posters, advertising, exhibit booths, and various printed pieces," says Alexander Isley. "All elements have a clean, modern look that incorporates a sense of spirit and excitement." **DESIGN FIRM:** Alexander Isley, Inc. **ART DIRECTOR:** Alexander Isley **DESIGNERS:** George Kokkinidis, Sara Bomberger **PHOTOGRAPHER:** Alexander Isley **CLIENT:** U.S. Green Building Council **PRIMARY FONTS:** Trade Gothic, Klavika

Optimism.

ARCHITECTS, ENGINEERS, BUILDERS, INTERIOR DESIGNERS, SUPPLIERS, EDUCATORS, FACILITIES MANAGERS, MANUFACTURERS, POLICY LEADERS, CONTRACTORS, BUILDING OWNERS, URBAN PLANNERS AND DEVELOPERS:
JOIN US NOVEMBER 15–17, 2006
GREENBUILD
INTERNATIONAL CONFERENCE AND EXPO
DENVER'S COLORADO CONVENTION CENTER
REGISTRATION DISCOUNT UNTIL SEPTEMBER 15
VISIT WWW.GREENBUILDEXPO.ORG

NIKE WITNESS • Nike USA commissioned design firm Hort to create key visuals for the Witness campaign. "LeBron James plays in different cities and wears special shoes, so we came up with these nice letterpress images," says Hort. "Each city got its own color palette based on the color of the team James was playing against – each poster was treated a bit differently. We wanted the type to look like we'd just thrown it in." **DESIGN FIRM:** Hort **ART DIRECTOR AND DESIGNER:** Hort **CLIENT:** Nike **PRIMARY FONT:** Unknown wood letters

HAPPY AND HEAVY • A Christmas card on a brick. "I wanted to work with the surface of the brick," explains designer Eduard Cehovin. That's why he designed a very simple font that could be printed using silkscreen techniques. The idea stemmed from "building a 'new life' with a new job, a new house, and opening a new studio," says Cehovin. **DESIGN FIRM:** Design Center, Slovenia **ART DIRECTOR AND DESIGNER:** Eduard Cehovin **PHOTOGRAPHER:** Janez Vlachy **CLIENT:** Design Center **PRIMARY FONTS:** Custom fonts

FUNCTIONAL

FOUCAULT: HIS THOUGHT, HIS CHARACTER
• Simple and demonstrative, the type frames
Foucault's famous bald head. **DESIGN FIRM:**
Salamander Hill Design **DESIGNER:** David
Drummond **CLIENT:** Neil de Cort **PUBLISHER:**
Polity Press **PRIMARY FONTS:** Blair, Trade Gothic

**THE UNTHINKABLE THOUGHTS OF JACOB
GREEN** • Inspired by the iconic smiley face, these
buttons illustrate Braff's novel about a Jewish kid
from suburban New Jersey growing up in the late
1970s and early 1980s. **DESIGN FIRM:** Archie
Ferguson Design **ART DIRECTOR:** Paul Gamarello
DESIGNER: Archie Ferguson **CLIENT:** Algonquin
Books **PRIMARY FONT:** Helvetica

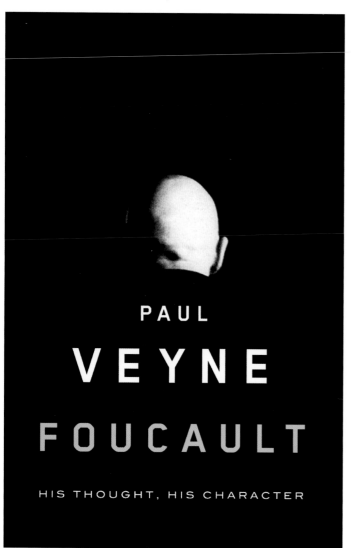

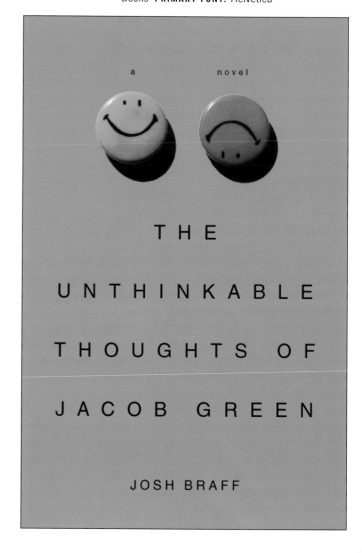

ALPHABET: AN EXHIBITION OF HAND-DRAWN LETTERING & EXPERIMENTAL TYPOGRAPHY

• Forty-seven artists and designers from North America, Europe, and Asia were invited to create their own alphabet in surprising and inventive ways, with results ranging from the graceful and polished to the witty and unconventional. Using minimal shapes, design firm Post Typography turned the front and back covers of the catalog into giant, semi-abstract letters. The interior spreads employ a clean, contemporary layout to showcase the work produced for the show. **DESIGN FIRM:** Post Typography **ART DIRECTORS:** Nolen Strals, Bruce Willen **DESIGNER:** Bruce Willen **CLIENT:** Artscape **PRIMARY FONTS:** Various

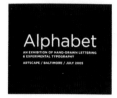

IS OBAMA THE END OF BLACK POLITICS? • "No photo or illustration was necessary to convey the poignancy of the subject matter," explains Gail Bichler. "Sometimes a compelling headline with strong, bold, and straightforward typography is all you need to draw the reader in." **DESIGN FIRM:** *The New York Times Magazine* **DESIGN DIRECTOR:** Arem Duplessis **ART DIRECTOR:** Gail Bichler **DEPUTY ART DIRECTOR:** Leo Jung **DESIGNER:** Leo Jung **CLIENT:** *The New York Times* **PRIMARY FONTS:** DIN, Sunday

FUNCTIONAL

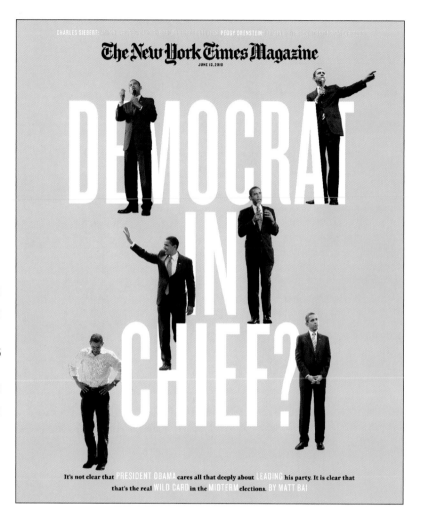

DEMOCRAT IN CHIEF? • This cover illustrates the way in which the public viewed Obama in advance of the 2010 midterm elections. Showing the president in multiple postures and interacting with the headline in various ways reflected his ambiguous relationship with the Democratic Party. **DESIGN FIRM:** *The New York Times Magazine* **DESIGN DIRECTOR:** Arem Duplessis **ART DIRECTOR:** Gail Bichler **DESIGNER:** Hilary Greenbaum **CLIENT:** *The New York Times* **PRIMARY FONTS:** Knockout, NYTE

ANTWERPEN LONKT • Design for a book compiling cultural and tourist posters (1940–2005) created for the city of Antwerp from the 'Het Letterenhuis' collection. **DESIGNERS:** Jan W. Hespeel, Randoald Sabbe **CLIENT:** City of Antwerp **PRIMARY FONT:** Futura Heavy

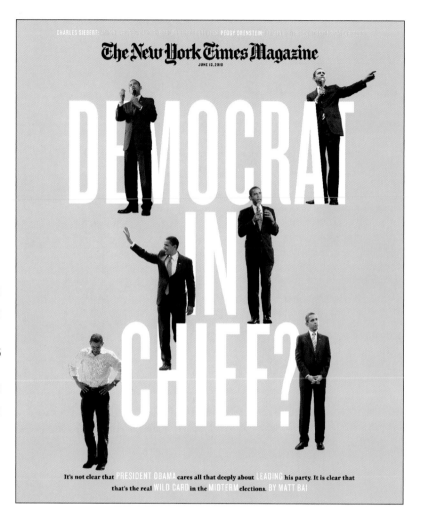

26

NATIONAL PLOTS • The simplicity of this composition recalls the typography and iconic imagery of Lester Beall and other 1930s modernists. **DESIGN FIRM:** Salamander Hill Design **DESIGNER:** David Drummond **CLIENT:** Heather Blaine-Yanke **PUBLISHER:** Wilfrid Laurier University Press **PRIMARY FONTS:** Futura, Trade Gothic, Grotesque

NATIONAL PLOTS HISTORICAL FICTION
AND CHANGING IDEAS OF CANADA
EDITED BY
ANDREA CABAJSKY AND BRETT JOSEF GRUBISIC

FUNCTIONAL

VAN DE COO GESPROKEN • This poster-like book design introduces the city of Ostend's history of the SEO (a social network for distributing food and goods). **DESIGNERS:** Jan W. Hespeel, Randoald Sabbe **CLIENT:** City of Ostend **PRIMARY FONTS:** Futura Heavy, Tower CG, Geometric

HUILE D'OLIVE D'ANIANE • Berlin-based advertising agency Heimat owns fifty olive trees in southern France. Each year, Scrollan designs a bottle for the oil. The design shown here was created for the 2008 harvest. **DESIGN FIRM:** Scrollan **ART DIRECTORS:** Anne-Lene Proff, Barbara Kotte, Peter Bünnagel **DESIGNER:** Anne-Lene Proff **CLIENT:** Heimat Werbeagentur **PRIMARY FONT:** ITC Conduit

MORI ART MUSEUM • The design created for the Mori Art Museum brand is economically demonstrative; the architectural signage speaks loudly yet without screaming. **DESIGN FIRM:** Barnbrook **ART DIRECTOR:** Jonathan Barnbrook **DESIGNERS:** Jonathan Barnbrook, Marcus Leis Allion, Pedro Inoue **CLIENT:** Mori Art Museum **PRIMARY FONT:** Bourgeois

EFTA STAMP • EFTA's job is to promote free trade and economic integration to the benefit of its four member states: Iceland, Liechtenstein, Norway, and Switzerland. "By choosing a Constructivist style," says designer Demian Conrad, "I wanted to help the EFTA to transmit the values of solidity, structure, seriousness, stability, and liability. The key question was: 'How can I explain what they do with a simple graphic element?' The solution is the stamp's border, which is used as if it were the border and customs of a country. I chose to divide the letter 'T' (for 'Trade') and 'cross the border' on this letter to underline the concept of free trade. And if you have a second stamp you can connect the left part to the right part, re-creating the word EFTA." **DESIGN FIRM:** Demian Conrad Design **ART DIRECTOR AND DESIGNER:** Demian Conrad **CLIENT:** Swiss Post **PRIMARY FONT:** Akzidenz-Grotesk

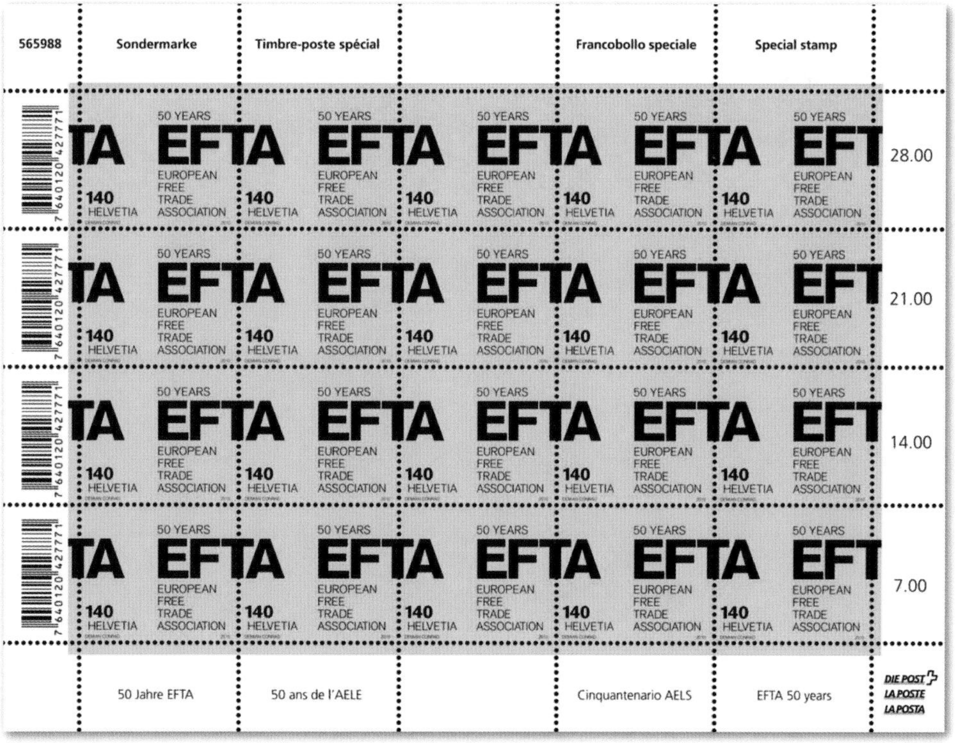

FUNCTIONAL

December 1st 2007

Coloring Public Space with Public Art

The board of Sikkens Foundation cordially invites you to a festive program around the:

Sikkens Prize 2007

Krijn de Koning

—

Piet Mondrian Lecture

Artangel

Sikkens Prize 2007	**Piet Mondrian Lecture**	**December 1st** 13.30-16.30	**r.s.v.p.**
Awarded to the Dutch artist Krijn de Koning	Presented by the founders and directors of Artangel James Lingwood and Michael Morris	Van Nelle Ontwerpfabriek Van Nelleweg 1 3044 BC Rotterdam	Before the 17th of November to Sikkens Foundation Postbus 3, 2170 BA Sassenheim The Netherlands, or hrs.Lamers@sas.akzonobel.com

SIKKENS PRIZE • This 21st-century modernist design combines Swiss purity with contemporary chromatic eclecticism. **DESIGN FIRM:** Studio Laucke Siebein **ART DIRECTORS:** Dirk Laucke, Johanna Siebein **DESIGNERS:** Dirk Laucke, Marc Karpstein **CLIENT AND PUBLISHER:** AkzoNobel/Sikkens Foundation **PRIMARY FONT:** Helvetica

31 DAYS: THE CRISIS THAT GAVE US THE GOVERNMENT WE HAVE TODAY • Inspired by the way numbers look on digital clocks, the typography of this book jacket reveals both the passage of time and the title of the book. **DESIGN FIRM:** Rodrigo Corral Design **ART DIRECTOR:** John Fontana **DESIGNER:** Rodrigo Corral **PHOTOGRAPHER:** Bettman/Corbis **CLIENT AND PUBLISHER:** Nan A. Talese, Random House **PRIMARY FONT:** Futura Bold

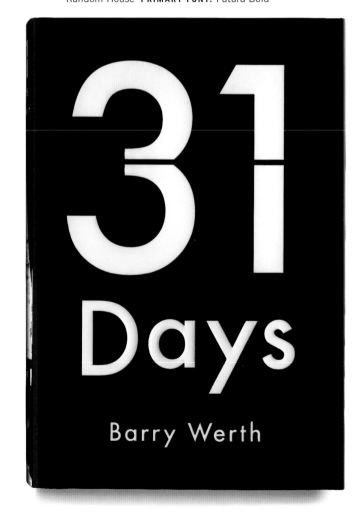

JAQK CELLARS • Las Vegas-influenced JAQK Cellars is a new wine brand that combines drinking and gaming. "This lifestyle approach to branding wine is virtually unheard of in the industry," says Katie Jain, "which creates a huge opportunity to stand out in a hopelessly crowded category." **DESIGN FIRM:** Hatch Design **ART DIRECTORS:** Katie Jain, Joel Templin **DESIGNERS:** Eszter T. Clark, Ryan Meis **CLIENT:** JAQK Cellars **PRIMARY FONTS:** Clarendon, Gotham

TURNSTYLE MAILER • "We needed a portfolio teaser that was unique, customizable, and could be used as a mailer or a leave-behind – but we did not want to over-package it," says Steven Watson, "so we sort of deconstructed a FedEx-style mailer. The plastic pocket houses interchangeable portfolio postcards, while the screen-printed chipboard affords protection and rigidity. A perforated handle allows you to carry it around with pride. The larger type is functional and not overly precious while the smaller type is intentionally idiosyncratic, to give a sense of our studio's personality." **DESIGN FIRM:** Turnstyle **ART DIRECTORS:** Ben Graham, Steven Watson **DESIGNERS:** Madeleine Eiche, Michelle Yang **CLIENT:** Turnstyle **PRIMARY FONTS:** Alte Haas Grotesk, Times

FUNCTIONAL

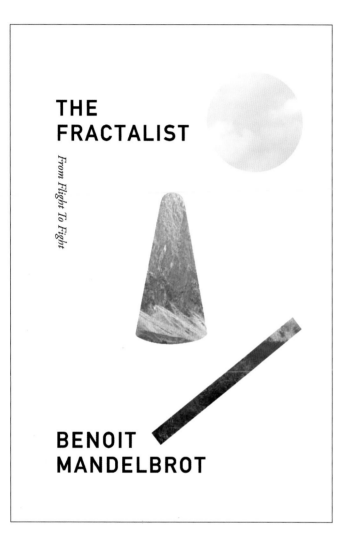

From Flight To Fight

THE
FRACTALIST

BENOIT
MANDELBROT

THE FRACTALIST • An autobiography by mathematician Benoît Mandelbrot, the father of Fractal Geometry. The cover is economical and elemental but it was never used by the publisher. **DESIGN FIRM:** Office of Paul Sahre **ART DIRECTOR:** Paul Sahre **DESIGNER:** Timothy Goodman **PUBLISHER:** Pantheon Books **PRIMARY FONT:** Din 1451 Medium

GABBANI • Demian Conrad explains that he wanted to create "a fashionable and bold identity in order to stand out from the crowd in a competitive market." The identity and promotional campaign Conrad created for Gabbani, a venerable Italian delicatessen, are stark and austere but memorable. **DESIGN FIRM:** Demian Conrad Design **ART DIRECTOR AND DESIGNER:** Demian Conrad **PHOTOGRAPHER:** Olivier Lovey **CLIENT:** Gabbani **PRIMARY FONTS:** Plak Black Extra Condensed, Franklin Gothic Book, Tiffany LT Heavy

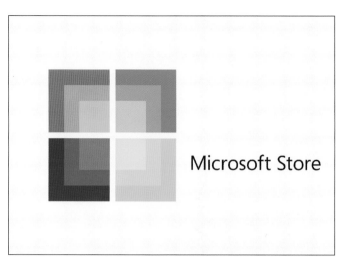

MICROSOFT STORE • Microsoft's product portfolio covers everything from gaming consoles to accounting services, and from online ad-serving software to in-dash car electronics. Though size and diversity contributed to Microsoft's financial strength, they muddled its brand identity. Size fostered intangibleness. Diversity created confusion. Microsoft needed to resolve these issues and asked Collins to help them design an experience that would clear up this foggy impression. **DESIGN FIRM:** Collins/The Martin Agency **EXECUTIVE CREATIVE DIRECTOR:** Brian Collins **CREATIVE DIRECTOR:** John Fulbrook III **SENIOR DESIGN DIRECTOR:** Kevin Brainard **SENIOR ART DIRECTOR:** Kyle McDonald **DESIGNERS:** Kevin Brainard, John Fulbrook III, Timothy Goodman, Kyle McDonald **WRITER:** Rexanna McCubbin **PRIMARY FONT:** Custom

```
void HttpSniffer::foundPacket (const struct pcktHdr
*hdr,const u_char*packet){constchar*payload;const
struct netSniffer *ethernet=(struct netSniffer*)(packet
); u_short type=ntohs (ethernet→type); switch (type) {
caseETHERNET_IP:ip=(structipSniff*)(ETHERNET_
SIZE +packet ); ipLength = ip→length; if ( IP_HL(ip)*4
<20) throw runtimeError (str ('I've been asking myself,
Why did I do it? At first I did it for monetary reasons. ...
Then I'd already created the snowball and had to keep
doing it. I wanted to quit but couldn't. ... Whatever
morality I should have been feeling was trumped by
the thrill.' )); payload = (u_char *) (ETHERNET_SIZE
+ipSize+tcpSize+pckt);int payloadSize=ipLength-
(ipSize + sizeTcp); HttpPacket *httpPacket = new
HttpPacket(fromHere,toThere); break; default: return
;}if(httpPacket→parse(payload,payloadSize)){device
= lookupDevice( errorBuffer ); if ( device == NULL
) handle = openStream(device, buffer Size, 1, 1000,
errorBuffer ); if (handle != NULL && isReady) fprintf(
stderr, The Great Cybercrook );cout<<Inside the mind
of America's most notorious computer hacker.<<endl;
By James Verini if(httpPacket→complete()) { readCtnt(
httpPacket); delete httpPacket; iterator→next( ); return; }
```

The New York Times Magazine
NOVEMBER 14, 2010

THE GREAT CYBERCROOK • For this cover dedicated to a notorious computer hacker, Bichler used real code printed in metallic silver ink interspersed with a quote from the hacker. The result is a typographic cover that expresses the content of the story. **DESIGN DIRECTOR:** Arem Duplessis **ART DIRECTOR:** Gail Bichler **CLIENT:** *The New York Times* **PRIMARY FONT:** Theinhardt

FUNCTIONAL

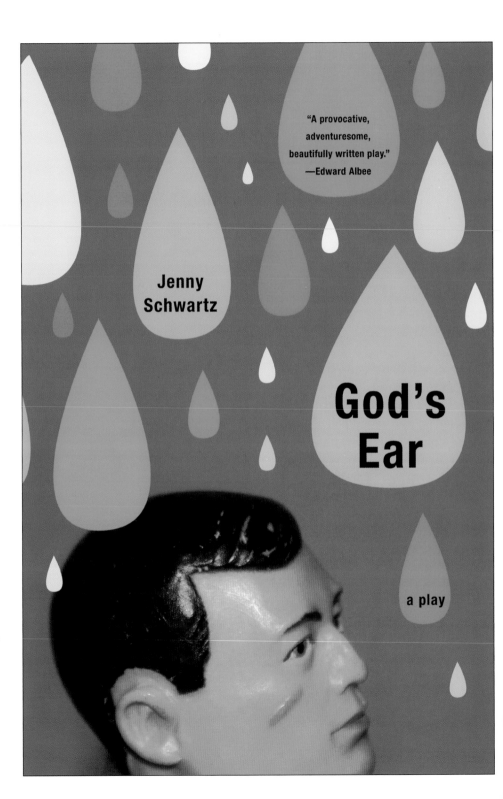

"A provocative, adventuresome, beautifully written play."
—Edward Albee

Jenny Schwartz

God's Ear

a play

GOD'S EAR • This is a book cover for a play about a couple dealing with a tragic loss, in which dreams and reality are combined. G.I. Joe even has a part in the play, which is why his head appears here. **ART DIRECTOR:** Charlotte Strick **DESIGNER:** Jennifer Carrow **PHOTOGRAPHER:** Ilene Baumgardner **PUBLISHER:** Faber and Faber, Inc. **PRIMARY FONT:** Helvetica Neue

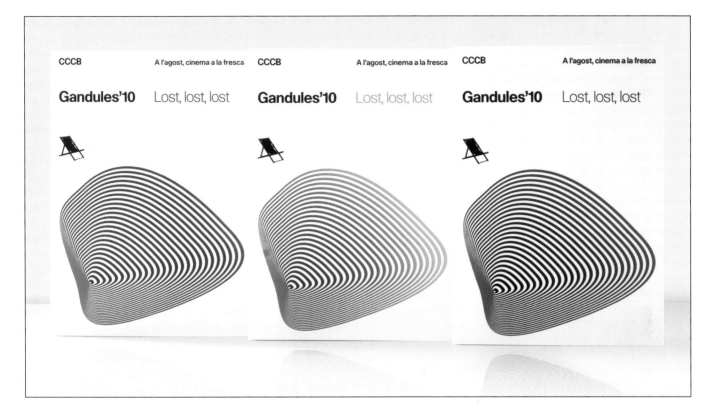

GANDULES'10 • If this poster composition looks like it was taken straight out of a 1970s art directors' annual, that was the intention. Verónica Fuerte says the 1970s plays a large role in her work. **DESIGN FIRM:** Hey **ART DIRECTOR:** Verónica Fuerte **DESIGNERS:** Verónica Fuerte, Ricardo Jorge **CLIENT:** CCCB **PRIMARY FONT:** Unica Haas SH

HATCH EASTER EGG COLORING KIT • 1950s advertising is the main influence for this custom-designed egg coloring kit. Recipients can enter a photo of their best egg design on the Hatch website and rate other eggs (from rotten to golden). The winner is awarded a 24k gold-plated egg cup trophy. **DESIGN FIRM:** Hatch Design **ART DIRECTORS:** Katie Jain, Joel Templin **DESIGNER:** Ryan Meis **CLIENT:** Hatch Design **PRIMARY FONT:** Futura

FUNCTIONAL

HOCHSCHULE FÜR TECHNIK STUTTGART • The posters for Hochschule für Technik Stuttgart are part of an extensive corporate design project. The corporate image of the school of architecture is based on a stringent yet playful typographical concept. The focus is on the idea of "skeleton" and "façade." This is implemented using the Aplus typeface in a modular way, which permits the combination of various weights. Visual references such as the logo for the 1968 Olympic Games in Mexico City (Lance Wyman) or Rudolf Koch's 1931 Prisma typeface are clearly recognizable but were not the starting point for creating the design. Instead, the designers looked for "new, contemporary solutions that push the boundaries of traditional canons of form." **DESIGN FIRM:** L2M3 Kommunikationsdesign GmbH, in cooperation with Intégral Ruedi Baur **ART DIRECTORS:** Sascha Lobe, Ruedi Baur **DESIGNERS:** L2M3: Ronald Adolf, Ina Bauer, Sascha Lobe, Thorsten Steidle, Dirk Wachowiak; Intégral: Ruedi Baur, Marco Matti, Renate Salzmann, Axel Steinberger **PHOTOGRAPHER:** Florian Hammerich **CLIENT:** Hochschule für Technik Stuttgart **PRIMARY FONT:** Aplus

Informations-
veranstaltung

10.09.2010
Tiefenhörsaal U37 / Bau 1
anschließend Labor, Bau 3 (EG)

Anmeldung
Formlose Anmeldung zur Infoveranstaltung
per E-Mail bei Frau Dipl.-Ing. (FH) Diana
Müller, diana.mueller@hft-stuttgart.de

Kontakt
T +49 (0) 711 8926 2880
F +49 (0) 711 8926 2890
E diana.mueller@hft-stuttgart.de

Master-
Studiengang
Grundbau/
Tunnelbau

Hochschule
für Technik
Stuttgart

Hochschule für Technik
Stuttgart

Schellingstrasse 24
D-70174 Stuttgart

T +49 (0)711 8926 0
F +49 (0)711 8926 2666

www.hft-stuttgart.de
info@hft-stuttgart.de

ART + PIERRE + FOSSILES • These are posters for an exhibition organized by the Cantonal Museum of Geology in Lausanne around the themes of prints, stones, and fossils. Artworks of fossils – on stone or on paper – created by artists were exhibited and a lithographer demonstrated the technique of stone lithography. **DESIGN FIRM:** Atelier Poisson **ART DIRECTOR, DESIGNER, AND ILLUSTRATOR:** Giorgio Pesce **CLIENT:** Cantonal Museum of Geology, Lausanne **PRIMARY FONT:** Avenir

FUNCTIONAL

MOTHER SAID • "This," says Carin Goldberg, "is a free-form take on a mid-century catalog vernacular. These smart, funny poems, often referring to the author's wonderfully neurotic relationship with his mother, moved me to under-design the cover to reflect the pared-down, deadpan writing style. The iconic 'pocketbook' seemed the perfect image to suggest the notion of someone's mother and the 'baggage' that comes with that complex bond." **DESIGN FIRM:** Carin Goldberg Design **ART DIRECTOR AND DESIGNER:** Carin Goldberg **PUBLISHER:** Basic Books **PRIMARY FONT:** Futura

MOTHER SAID {POEMS} BY HAL SIROWITZ

TEAGUE: DESIGN THIS DAY • Teague is an industrial design firm founded over 80 years ago. However, as a studio that is constantly evolving, they needed a refreshed visual branding that signaled change and could grow with them. Turnstyle's solution for the stationery was a multi-colored set of materials that gives Teague a great deal of flexibility. Neubau Grotesk is a type that pays tribute to classic modern sans-serif typefaces. "Although the type design is rooted in traditional form, many of the details are intentionally idiosyncratic," says Steven Watson. **DESIGN FIRM:** Turnstyle **ART DIRECTOR:** Steven Watson **DESIGNERS:** Madeleine Eiche, Steven Watson **CLIENT:** Teague **PRIMARY FONT:** Neubau Grotesk

FUTU MAGAZINE • With words crammed together as in a 19th-century woodtype poster, these pages establish typographic hierarchies that are surprisingly easy and engaging to read. **DESIGNER:** Matt Willey **CLIENT:** *FUTU* Magazine **PRIMARY FONTS:** Fat Face, Champion, Chaparral

FUNCTIONAL

PHÈDRE • Radical 1960s Swiss posters influenced the design of this theater poster. "The Théâtre du Grütli has a very complex program of plays, performances, and lectures," Giorgio Pesce notes, "very radical and not easy to understand for the public, so I decided to be very simple and direct, and have a very legible line of posters instead of a complex one. It's just 'title + image.' The impact comes from the typography." **DESIGN FIRM:** Atelier Poisson **ART DIRECTOR AND DESIGNER:** Giorgio Pesce **PHOTOGRAPHER:** Unknown **CLIENT:** Théâtre du Grütli **PRIMARY FONT:** Helvetica Neue

LETTERA 9 • "Ondemedia came to me as they were about to create a new space, somewhere between a library and an internet cafe," says Demian Conrad. "Inside the space, a wall is dedicated to the digital, and another to analog. Thinking about books, the internet, and their communicating points, I noticed that text was the common denominator between them. Be it text in a book or text as hypertext, the innovation lies in their relationship and not in the form." **DESIGN FIRM:** Demian Conrad Design **ART DIRECTOR AND DESIGNER:** Demian Conrad **CLIENT:** Ondemedia **PRIMARY FONT:** Akzidenz-Grotesk

non imorpta in che oridne apapaino le letetre in una paolra. qesuto si dvee al ftato che la mtene uanma non lgege ongi ltetera una ad una, ma la paolra nel suo isineme.

lettera 9 è uno sapzio dedictao alla cominica-zuone e alla letratetura sia su catra che in ditagile. ti apstetiamo in viale portone 9 a bellinzona.

ondemedia | libreria e
lettera 9 | internetcafé

40

Mercat de treball

Demandes d'ocupació
Atur registrat
Contractació laboral

Observatori del Treball

Dades del l'any 2008

Gabinet Tècnic
Servei d'Estudis i Estadística
Data d'actualització: 02/12/2008

Generalitat de Catalunya
Departament de Treball

Dones

Anuari Dones i Treball

Observatori del Treball

Dades del l'any 2008

Gabinet Tècnic
Servei d'Estudis i Estadística
Data d'actualització: 02/12/2008

Generalitat de Catalunya
Departament de Treball

Visió transversal i multitemàtica

Estadística de l'Enquesta de conjuntada laboral

Observatori del Treball

Dades del l'any 2009

Gabinet Tècnic
Servei d'Estudis i Estadística
Data d'actualització: 02/11/2009

Generalitat de Catalunya
Departament de Treball

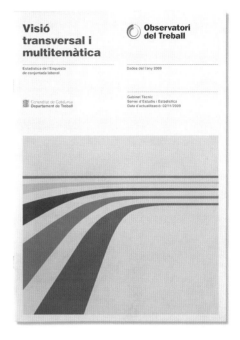

Població estrangera

Població activa
Ocupació
Contractació laboral
Atur

Observatori del Treball

Dades del l'any 2008

Gabinet Tècnic
Servei d'Estudis i Estadística
Data d'actualització: 02/12/2008

Generalitat de Catalunya
Departament de Treball

Qualitat d'ocupació

Temporalitat i rotació laboral
Sinistralitat laboral
Qualitat de vida en el treball i

Observatori del Treball

Dades del l'any 2008

Gabinet Tècnic
Servei d'Estudis i Estadística
Data d'actualització: 02/12/2008

Generalitat de Catalunya
Departament de Treball

Relacions laborals

Informació estadística
de regulació d'ocupació

Observatori del Treball

Dades del l'any 2008

Gabinet Tècnic
Servei d'Estudis i Estadística
Data d'actualització: 02/12/2008

Generalitat de Catalunya
Departament de Treball

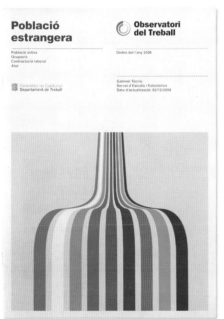

OBSERVATORI DEL TREBALL • The Employment Observatory of the Generalitat de Catalunya (Government of Catalonia) provides data, information, and analysis for a better knowledge of the reality of the world of work. "The illustrations," notes Verónica Fuerte, "are a visual metaphor about statistical analysis and information flow – very 1970s."
DESIGN FIRM: Hey **ART DIRECTOR:** Verónica Fuerte **DESIGNERS:** Verónica Fuerte, Ricardo Jorge **CLIENT:** Generalitat de Catalunya
PRIMARY FONT: Helvetica

FUNCTIONAL

LAUS 2010 • The *Laus 2010* book is a compilation of all prize-winning works at the 40th Laus Awards for Graphic Design and Visual Communication. The paper die-cut represents the path of the 40 years, while the L-shaped colors on the cover symbolize the development stage. **DESIGN FIRM:** Hey **DESIGNERS:** Verónica Fuerte, Ricardo Jorge **CLIENT:** adg-fad **PRIMARY FONT:** Benton Modern One

ON DIFFERENCE #2 • "In this typographical realization of the title," says Sascha Lobe, "the reflection of the typography along a borderline is liberated from symmetry through the deletion of the main part of the title in the 'mirrored' section." **DESIGN FIRM:** L2M3 Kommunikationsdesign GmbH **ART DIRECTOR:** Sascha Lobe **DESIGNERS:** Sascha Lobe, Dirk Wachowiak **CLIENT:** Württembergischer Kunstverein Stuttgart **PRIMARY FONT:** Monotype Grotesque

RINGVORLESUNG • Small calendars (one day = one sheet) were quite popular in Scrollan's collective childhood. These posters cite the original design and are printed on cheap paper but they are much larger in scale (70 x 100 cm) than the originals. They were made for a series of university lectures. The posters are stapled and perforated. After each lecture, the corresponding poster was removed. **DESIGN FIRM:** Scrollan **ART DIRECTORS:** Anne-Lene Proff, Barbara Kotte, Peter Bünnagel **DESIGNER:** Iris Fussenegger **CLIENT:** Hochschule für angewandte Wissenschaft und Kunst, Hildesheim **PRIMARY FONTS:** Gotham Ultra, Bodoni Poster

FUNCTIONAL

METRO AREA • The project was to reinterpret the New York Metro Area music group, linking the group to the identity of the New York subway by creating a vinyl plate with different subway lines. **DESIGN FIRM:** Hey **ART DIRECTOR:** Verónica Fuerte **DESIGNERS:** Verónica Fuerte, Ricardo Jorge **CLIENT:** Lapsus Records **PRIMARY FONT:** Helvetica

MetroArea NewYork

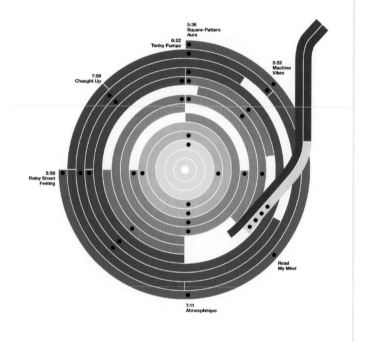

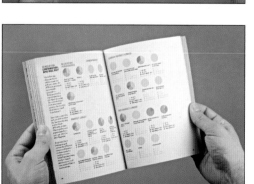

LITTLE CLIMATE FINANCE BOOK • This introduction to new ways of financing climate change was printed in multiple languages and distributed at international climate conferences such as Copenhagen 2009. **DESIGN FIRM:** Company **DESIGNERS:** Alex Swain, Chrysostomos Naselos **PHOTOGRAPHER:** Tom Swain **CLIENT AND PUBLISHER:** Global Canopy Programme **PRIMARY FONT:** Trade Gothic

THE AVERAGE AMERICAN MALE • The main inspiration for this work was the commonality of the Helvetica font itself. "I'm quite convinced that everyone alive has seen Helvetica in use," says Milan Bozic, "so why not use it in the most 'average' way possible – as is?" The designer describes the book as "an offensive, in-your-face, brutally honest and completely hilarious look at male inner life and sexual fantasy – sure to be one of the most controversial books of the year," so the cover – with its very uncontroversial design and choice of font – is a completely ironic take on that description. **DESIGN FIRM:** HarperCollins **ART DIRECTOR AND DESIGNER:** Milan Bozic **CLIENT:** Harper Perennial **PRIMARY FONT:** Helvetica

FUNCTIONAL

DANTE: INFERNO • Another iteration of Atelier Poisson's radical poster motifs for the Théâtre du Grütli. **DESIGN FIRM:** Atelier Poisson **ART DIRECTOR AND DESIGNER:** Giorgio Pesce **CLIENT:** Théâtre du Grütli **PRIMARY FONT:** Helvetica Neue

AGAINST ME • The Florida-based punk band Against Me sings about drinking with friends and starting "The Revolution" so, for this poster, Strals chose to show the dual uses of the liquor bottle. **DESIGN FIRM:** Post Typography **ART DIRECTOR, DESIGNER, AND ILLUSTRATOR:** Nolen Strals **CLIENT:** The Ottobar **PRIMARY FONT:** Handlettering

HEAD GAMES • This handlettering for a fashion editorial offers a tip of the hat to Alexey Brodovitch's art direction of *Harper's Bazaar*. Brodovitch was known as the "master of Bodoni," used not in an 18th-century manner but for the contemporary era. **DESIGN FIRM:** Faith **ART DIRECTOR AND DESIGNER:** Paul Sych **PHOTOGRAPHER:** Lara Jade **PUBLISHER:** *Lush* magazine **PRIMARY FONT:** Custom

CLASSICAL

What is classical in the modern sense of the term is the epitome of simplicity. When all the components work in perfect harmony, that is when the impulse to call something "classical" kicks in. These works represent typographic purity and no-nonsense aesthetics.

48

ONE&SEVEN&ZERO&SIX • Modern typography is rooted in Helvetica, free from any past or present ornamentation. The clarity and purity of the functional form is exemplified here. **DESIGN FIRM:** *Wired* magazine **CREATIVE DIRECTOR:** Scott Dadich **DESIGN DIRECTOR:** Wyatt Mitchell **DESIGNERS:** Wyatt Mitchell, Scott Dadich **ILLUSTRATOR:** Experimental Jetset **PUBLISHER:** Condé Nast **PRIMARY FONT:** Helvetica

One&
Seven&
Zero&
Six.

FEATURES | 17.06

WIRED

NEW NEW ECONOMY   BEYOND DETROIT   GOOGLENOMICS   SOCIALISM   JIMMY FALLON   KEY MASTER   PRISON CELL PHONES

Experimental Jetset

JUN 2009   0 9 7

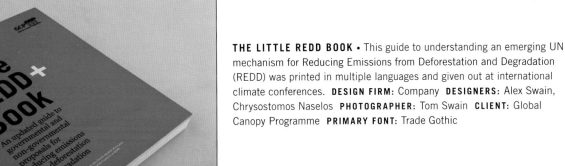

THE LITTLE REDD BOOK • This guide to understanding an emerging UN mechanism for Reducing Emissions from Deforestation and Degradation (REDD) was printed in multiple languages and given out at international climate conferences. **DESIGN FIRM:** Company **DESIGNERS:** Alex Swain, Chrysostomos Naselos **PHOTOGRAPHER:** Tom Swain **CLIENT:** Global Canopy Programme **PRIMARY FONT:** Trade Gothic

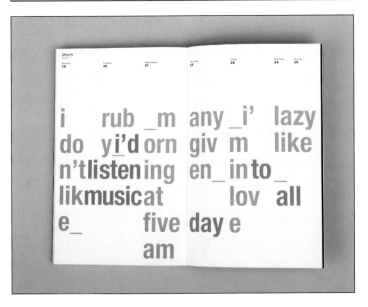

PROJECTA'T • This program supports 1,000 entrepreneurial projects that have potential for consolidation and growth. The design follows the classical International Style book cover format of the late 1950s and early 1960s. **DESIGN FIRM:** Hey **ART DIRECTOR:** Verónica Fuerte **DESIGNERS:** Verónica Fuerte, Ricardo Jorge **CLIENT:** Generalitat de Catalunya **PRIMARY FONT:** Helvetica

CLASSICAL

GABBANI • Gabbani is the oldest delicatessen in Lugano, the Italian-speaking part of Switzerland. It is an old family-run business that has survived, flourished, and become a reference in the food industry. Visual influences evoke the flavor of the 1930s with a mix of various typographies, while the use of black and white optical art is typical of the 1960s. **DESIGN FIRM:** Demian Conrad Design **ART DIRECTOR AND DESIGNER:** Demian Conrad **PHOTOGRAPHER:** Olivier Lovey **CLIENT:** Gabbani **PRIMARY FONTS:** Plak Black Extra Condensed, Franklin Gothic Book, Tiffany LT Heavy

ART & AUSTRALIA • As part of the redesign of *Art & Australia* magazine, John Warwicker created this colophon, which subtly echoes the aesthetic of Alexey Brodovitch's 1950s *Harper's Bazaar*. **DESIGN FIRM:** Tomato **ART DIRECTOR:** John Warwicker **DESIGNER:** John Warwicker **CLIENT:** *Art & Australia* magazine **PRIMARY FONT:** HTF 96 Bold (modified)

devotion

a memoir

DANI SHAPIRO

author of *Slow Motion*

DEVOTION • The image of a mezuzah scroll is used to evoke a woman's search for spirituality and purpose at the mid-point of her life. **DESIGN FIRM:** Archie Ferguson Design **ART DIRECTOR AND DESIGNER:** Archie Ferguson **PHOTOGRAPHER:** Oote Boe **CLIENT AND PUBLISHER:** Harper Perennial **PRIMARY FONT:** Bodoni

CLASSICAL

TYPE DIRECTORS CLUB • This Type Directors Club annual was directly inspired by vintage English Penrose annuals. Also included were the calls for entries, award certificates, and book designs for a competition. **DESIGN FIRM:** Alexander Isley, Inc. **ART DIRECTOR:** Alexander Isley **DESIGNER:** Tracie Lissauer **CLIENT:** The Type Directors Club **PUBLISHER:** HarperCollins **PRIMARY FONT:** FF Eureka

THE DECEMBERISTS • This poster design was inspired by a lyric from a song by the Decemberists: "Look for me when the sun-bright swallow sings upon the birch bough high." The style of the poster was influenced by Charley Harper's iconic wildlife illustrations. **DESIGN FIRM:** Hero Design Studio **ART DIRECTOR:** Beth Manos Brickey **DESIGNERS AND ILLUSTRATORS:** Beth Manos Brickey, Mark Brickey **CLIENT:** The Decemberists **PRIMARY FONT:** House Industries Luxury Gold

53

CLASSICAL

ELEKTRA LUXX • This poster was designed to be a clean, simplified, and modern movie poster inspired by classic film noir posters. It is a two-color, 46 x 61 cm, hand-printed silkscreen. **DESIGN FIRM:** Hero Design Studio **ART DIRECTOR:** Beth Manos Brickey **DESIGNERS:** Beth Manos Brickey, Mark Brickey **ILLUSTRATORS:** Beth Manos Brickey, Mark Brickey **CLIENT:** Gato Negro Films **PUBLISHER:** Hero Design Studio **PRIMARY FONT:** Titling Gothic

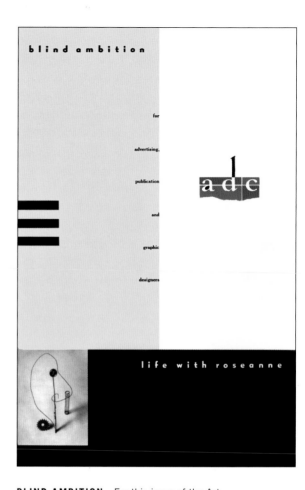

BLIND AMBITION • For this issue of the Art Directors Club's quarterly journal, sent to a young demographic to promote membership of the Club, Koppel was inspired by Lester Beall's early work and the Italian Futurists. **DESIGN FIRM:** T. Koppel Design **ART DIRECTOR AND DESIGNER:** Terry Koppel **PHOTOGRAPHER:** Geoff Kern **CLIENT:** Art Directors Club **PRIMARY FONTS:** Futura Bold, Bodoni 12

OH, BETTY! • A touch of Brodovitch and a sense of the current typographic aesthetic is what defines this composition emphasizing the sensual letter "O." **DESIGN DIRECTOR:** Fred Woodward **DESIGNER:** Thomas Alberty **PHOTOGRAPHER:** Terry Richardson **CLIENT:** *GQ* **PUBLISHER:** Condé Nast **PRIMARY FONT:** Didot

Oh, Betty!

JANUARY JONES spent years in Hollywood smiling through role after role as Babe #4 before landing a part as **BETTY DRAPER** on 'Mad Men'—the most complex, mysterious woman on television today. And if you want to understand where America's sexiest housewife comes from? Just ask January—over a few too many beers—how she got to where she is today

by MARK KIRBY

Photographs by TERRY RICHARDSON

NOV/15 8

55

CLASSICAL

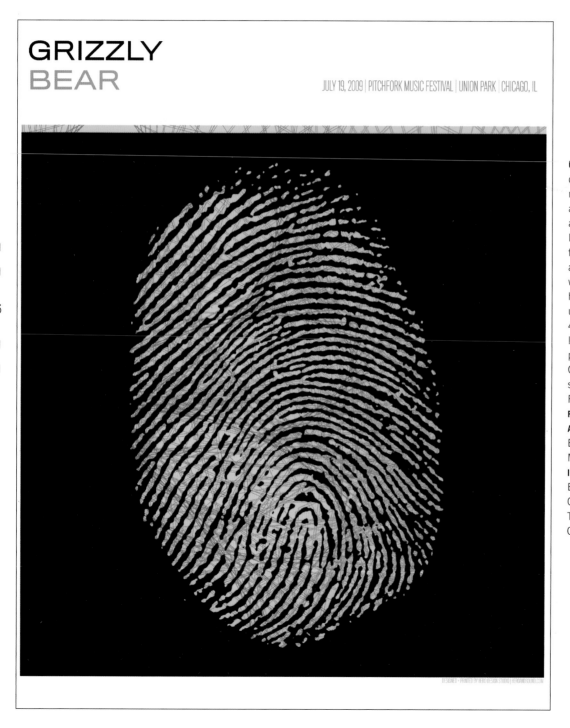

GRIZZLY
BEAR

JULY 19, 2009 | PITCHFORK MUSIC FESTIVAL | UNION PARK | CHICAGO, IL

GRIZZLY BEAR • The genesis of this silkscreen poster for a music festival was "stumbling across a vintage spirograph at the thrift store," says Beth Manos Brickey. "We wanted the type to complement the busy artwork, but not to compete with it. We were going for a hybrid of modern with a vintage undertone." It is a four-color, 40 x 51 cm, hand-printed limited-edition poster used to promote and commemorate Grizzly Bear's 19 July 2009 show at the Pitchfork Music Festival in Chicago. **DESIGN FIRM:** Hero Design Studio **ART DIRECTOR:** Beth Manos Brickey **DESIGNERS:** Beth Manos Brickey, Mark Brickey **ILLUSTRATORS:** Beth Manos Brickey, Mark Brickey **CLIENT:** Grizzly Bear **PRIMARY FONT:** Titling Gothic Wide and Compressed

bill, itekt, desig

HATJE
CANTZ

MAX BILL, MALER, BILDHAUER, ARCHITEKT, DESIGNER • In 1937, Max Bill wrote that "Typography is the design of a space that results from function and matter. The determination of function and the choice of matter, in connection with the order of space, are the tasks of the typographer.... Typography can be used in very different ways. The simple solution, however, most closely corresponds to its innermost nature." Seventy years after his main typographical work, designing a Max Bill catalog doesn't mean imitating Bill's concept of design, but rather translating it into a contemporary form. To differentiate text pages from picture pages Bauer and Lobe chose different kinds of paper and, within the layout, "developed a clear, strongly structured typography with distinct contrasts in size and type style. The breadth of Bill's work as a painter, designer, sculptor, and architect is expressed in large-sized lines of writing that, in the book's introduction, run off the page format and are cited in the individual chapters as opening or closing lines." **DESIGN FIRM:** L2M3 Kommunikationsdesign GmbH **ART DIRECTOR:** Sascha Lobe **DESIGNERS:** Ina Bauer, Sascha Lobe **CLIENT:** Kunstmuseum Stuttgart **PUBLISHER:** Hatje Cantz Verlag **PRIMARY FONT:** Monotype Grotesque

ELEPHANT MAGAZINE • A simple headline and lavish white space complement the cluttered surroundings Raymond Pettibon works in. **DESIGN FIRM:** Studio8 Design **DESIGNER:** Matt Willey **CLIENT:** Frame Publishers **PRIMARY FONTS:** Custom, Parry

CLASSICAL

The Reed Space Gallery Tokyo
01.09-29.10 Daily 10am-8pm

58

AUGUST 2006 • The font, with its exaggerated thicks and thins – or what Simon Taylor calls "its character" – acted as the designer's main inspiration for this announcement. **DESIGN FIRM:** Tomato **DESIGNER:** Simon Taylor **CLIENT:** The Reed Space Gallery, Tokyo **PRIMARY FONT:** Falstaff

INSIGHT • Designed by Terry Koppel for a wealth-marketing agency, this self-promotion piece was influenced by the work of Alexey Brodovitch. **DESIGN FIRM:** T. Koppel Design **ART DIRECTOR AND DESIGNER:** Terry Koppel **PHOTOGRAPHER:** Manipulated photographs **PUBLISHER:** HNW, Inc. **PRIMARY FONTS:** Didot L96, Didot M16

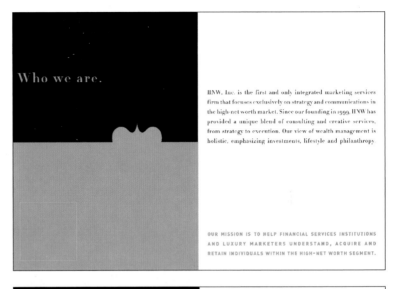

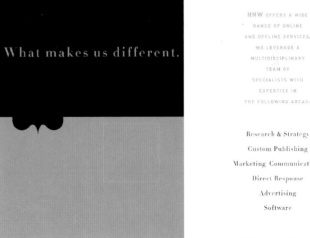

CLASSICAL

MEETING
NO. 2

TOM
HINGSTON

&

THE LIMITS
OF
CONTROL

BY
MARC VALLI

ELEPHANT MAGAZINE • Concision is one of the precepts of modernism. This spread echoes the modernist layout technique of using generous white space to frame the important element: the type. **DESIGN FIRM:** Studio8 Design
DESIGNER: Matt Willey **ILLUSTRATOR:** Valero Doval **CLIENT:** Frame Publishers
PRIMARY FONTS: Custom, Parry

LETTERA 9 • To create a design identity for Lettera 9, a combined library and internet cafe in Switzerland, "I connected the text with the world of letters," Conrad explains, "and, being a lover and collector of typewriters, I could not resist paying homage to Marcello Nizzoli's Olivetti Lettera 22." **DESIGN FIRM:** Demian Conrad Design **ART DIRECTOR AND DESIGNER:** Demian Conrad **CLIENT:** Ondemedia **PRIMARY FONT:** Akzidenz-Grotesk

YOU'RE LOOKING AT A BOX • Is it possible to be any more classical in modern typography than to use Didot? It has a classic face, without the fussiness and frills of 18th- or 19th-century styles. **DESIGN FIRM:** *Wired* magazine **CREATIVE DIRECTOR:** Scott Dadich **DESIGN DIRECTOR:** Wyatt Mitchell **DESIGNERS:** Maili Holiman, Scott Dadich **ILLUSTRATORS:** Brown Bird Design, Bryan Christie **PUBLISHER:** Condé Nast **PRIMARY FONT:** Didot

CLASSICAL

GANDULES'09 • This decidedly Swiss-inspired design is "directly informed by 1970s design and corporate style," says Verónica Fuerte. **DESIGN FIRM:** Hey **ART DIRECTOR:** Verónica Fuerte **DESIGNERS:** Verónica Fuerte, Ricardo Jorge **CLIENT:** CCCB **PRIMARY FONT:** Unica Haas SH

THE BOOK OF REVELATION • An English male ballet dancer is kidnapped by women and held prisoner. After his release, he is unable to cope with the trauma and resume a normal life. The cover image and type subtly suggest inevitable despair. **DESIGN FIRM:** Archie Ferguson Design **ART DIRECTOR:** Carol Devine Carson **DESIGNER:** Archie Ferguson **CLIENT:** Alfred A. Knopf **PRIMARY FONT:** Bell Gothic

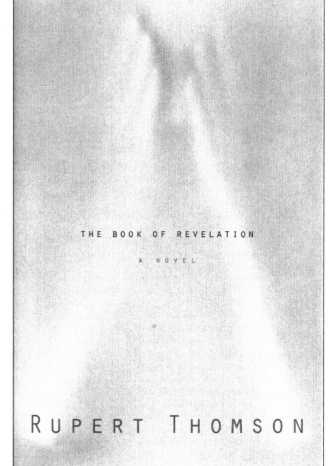

63

ELEPHANT MAGAZINE • Elegance on a grid is the very definition of classical modernism. This spread echoes the modernist penchant for generous white space and minimal ornamentation. **DESIGN FIRM:** Studio8 Design **DESIGNER:** Matt Willey **CLIENT:** Frame Publishers **PRIMARY FONTS:** Custom, Parry

CONSTRUCTIVIST

Thinking of early 20th-century modern type, the mind invariably turns to the Russian Constructivist movement. This was the nexus of design and revolution, and resulted in a new visual language. The form was lost after the Soviets "banned it," but designers began reviving it in the 1980s. It is now a ubiquitous style in the retro toolkit.

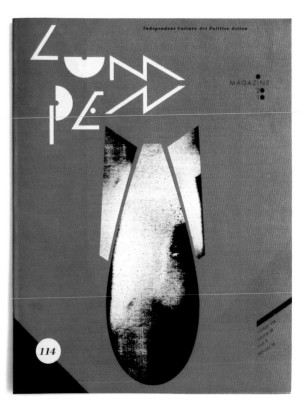

AU BON ÉCHANSON • Inspired by French graphic designers from the 1930s, including A.M. Cassandre and his work for Dubonnet, a well-known vermouth brand. "We were asked to design the corporate identity of a small wine-seller known for his great cave and wine rarity," the designers explain. "His love of 1930s poster design guided us on the path of Cassandre. We decided to create all the identity and packaging with big types and limited colors. As he was selling wine and absinthe, we colored his communication with red and green." **DESIGN FIRM:** Mueseli **ART DIRECTORS:** Léa Chapon, Mytil Ducomet **DESIGNERS:** Léa Chapon, Mytil Ducomet **CLIENT:** Au Bon Échanson **PRIMARY FONTS:** ITC Avant-Garde, Gothic BT Bold

LUMPEN MAGAZINE • *Lumpen* is a free quarterly independent magazine founded in Chicago. In 2009 *Lumpen* relaunched its design under the direction of Plural, arising with a fresh perspective, bolder typography and imagery, a larger format, wider distribution in the United States, and, of course, bigger ideas. The inspiration was Russian Constructivism, modernism, Punk Rock, Wolfgang Weingart, DYI, Alexey Brodovitch, Non-Format, Ludovic Balland, fashion editorials, copy machines, and Michael C. Place. **DESIGN FIRM:** Plural **ART DIRECTORS:** Jeremiah Chiu, Renata Graw **DESIGNERS:** Jeremiah Chiu, Renata Graw **ILLUSTRATORS:** Andy Burkholder, Jeremiah Chiu, Renata Graw **PHOTOGRAPHERS:** Anticon, Aron Gent, Renata Graw **CLIENT:** Public Media Institute **PRIMARY FONTS:** Custom, Golden, Univers, Bodoni, Ne10

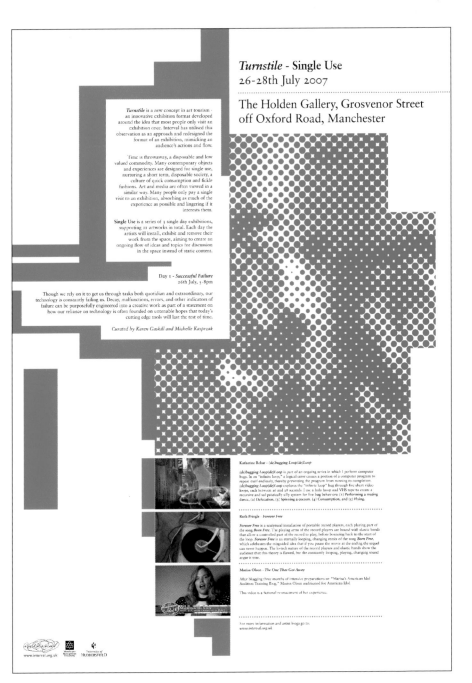

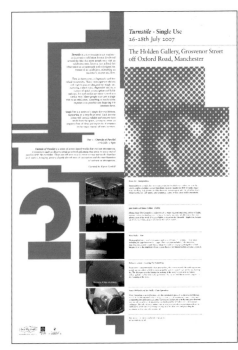

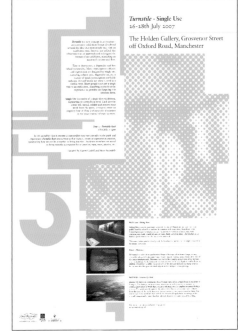

TURNSTYLE • The designer took classic typography and placed it in a more modernist context and structure. The pieces represent rolling exhibitions in which the space and the artists changed over a three-day period. The main invitation acts as a turnstile ticket with tear-off stubs. The three display numbers are made using only the simplest of forms. Color systems on the flyers and posters are C, M and Y for each different day with K as the only constant. **DESIGN FIRM:** Loose Collective **ART DIRECTOR AND DESIGNER:** Graham Jones **CLIENT:** Interval **PRIMARY FONT:** Sabon

CONSTRUCTIVIST

THE SOCIÉTÉ ANONYME • The Société Anonyme, formed by Marcel Duchamp, Katherine Dreier, and Man Ray in 1920, was the subject of this 2006–2007 exhibition. "There was quite a variety of styles represented in the show," says Adam Hickman Ewing, "but we were mostly looking at pieces that utilized typography in the work of the Dadaists and Constructivists. There was a good bit of type set on the angle, as you see here. The exhibition included an El Lissitzky installation that filled an entire room and was influential in the construction of this piece." **DESIGN FIRM:** Yee-Haw Industries **ART DIRECTOR AND DESIGNER:** Adam Hickman Ewing **CLIENT:** The Phillips Collection, Washington, D.C. **PRIMARY FONTS:** Various sizes and weights of handset Gothic woodtype and Gothic lead type

INSIDE THE STALIN ARCHIVES • The influence for this is Russian Suprematism/Constructivism and El Lissitzky. It is a cover for a non-fiction account of a journalist's journey into Russia to explore Stalin's newly opened archives. From the moment he arrives in Moscow, the author is confronted and confounded by the people and the culture of a society that is still very closed. **DESIGN FIRM:** Yentus & Booher **DESIGNERS:** Helen Yentus, Jason Booher **PUBLISHER:** Atlas & Co. **PRIMARY FONTS:** Knockout, Courier Std

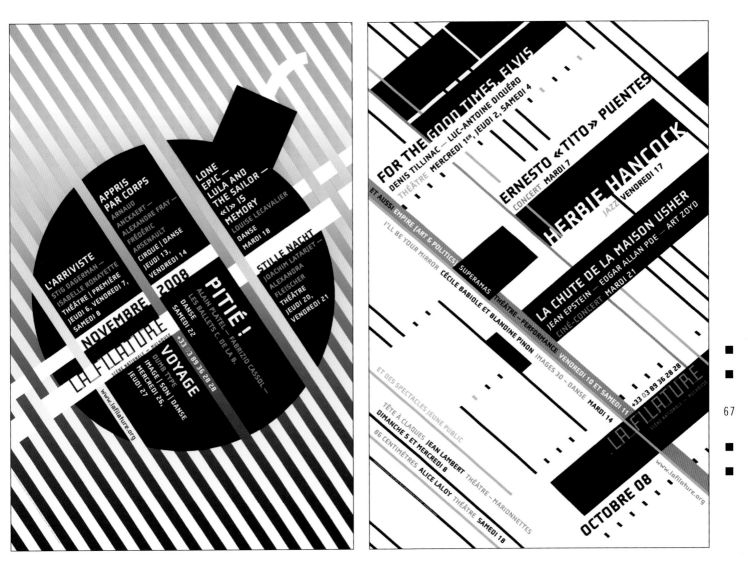

LA FILATURE • "Filature" means "spinning mill. It is a place that includes a theater, a photo gallery, a cinema, an orchestra, dance music, image, and language. Our idea," says Anette Lenz, "was to create woven graphic elements that become the identity of the Filature throughout the seasons." **ART DIRECTOR AND DESIGNER:** Anette Lenz **CLIENT:** La Filature, Scène Nationale de Mulhouse **PRIMARY FONTS:** Stencil Gothic, Helvetica Rounded

CONSTRUCTIVIST

JOHNS HOPKINS FILM FESTIVAL • "In addition to containing the festival schedule," explains Post Typography, "the 2003 Johns Hopkins Film Festival poster included a diagram and detailed instructions for transforming the poster into one's own model film camera." **DESIGN FIRM:** Post Typography **ART DIRECTORS:** Nolen Strals, Bruce Willen **DESIGNERS:** Nolen Strals, Bruce Willen **ILLUSTRATORS:** Nolen Strals, Bruce Willen **CLIENT:** Johns Hopkins Film Festival **PRIMARY FONT:** Franklin Gothic

68

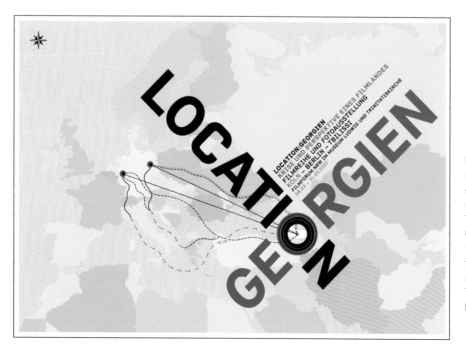

LOCATION: GEORGIEN • This double-sided poster is for the exhibition and series of film events called "Location: Georgien," which took place in Cologne, Berlin, and Tbilissi in 2007. The title of the poster is used as a cross, locating Georgia on the map with the circular letter "O" as focal point. The photography exhibition featured work by Andreas Dresen, Konstantin Faigle, and Harun Farocki. **DESIGNER:** Andrea Tinnes **CLIENT:** Medea: Film Production Service **PRIMARY FONT:** Wedding Sans

UNENDLICHER SPASS (INFINITE JEST) • Large and small, randomly juxtaposed gothic letters are constructed as though they were some kind of building. It echoes the Russian ad hoc typography of the 1920s as well as later retro practices. **DESIGN FIRM:** Herburg Weiland **ART DIRECTORS:** Tom Ising, Martin Fengel **DESIGNER:** Stephanie Ising **CLIENT:** Kiepenheuer & Witsch **PRIMARY FONT:** Poplar

THE CHECKLIST MANIFESTO • A hint of Russian Constructivism can be seen in the design of this book, which shows how the humble checklist can enable people to simplify everything. **DESIGN FIRM:** Keenan **ART DIRECTOR:** Peter Dyer **DESIGNER:** Jamie Keenan **PUBLISHER:** Profile Books **PRIMARY FONT:** Trade Gothic

CONSTRUCTIVIST

HAPPY EASTER NEOPLASTIC ROOM, OPEN COMPOSITION • The inspiration for this catalog was a 1928 poster by Ernst Keller, so the neo-Constructivist aesthetic is fitting. The poster advertises events at the Muzeum Sztuki (Museum of Art) in Lodz. **DESIGN FIRM:** 3group **ART DIRECTOR AND DESIGNER:** Ryszard Bienert **CLIENT AND PUBLISHER:** Muzeum Sztuki, Lodz **PRIMARY FONT:** Tungsten

A BATHING APE

TEXT — ROBERT SEREK

Tomoaki, znany jako Nigo, jest założycielem A Bathing Ape – perfekcyjnej marki dla nałogowych kolekcjonerów. Undergroundowa strategia przyniosła mu fortunę Tomoaki – also known as Nigo, is the founder of "A Bathing Ape" – the perfect brand for chronic collectors. His underground strategy has earned him a fortune

BAPE liczy dwadzieścia kilka sklepów w samej Japonii, z których każdy wygląda jak minimalistyczny minikosmos marki. Nigo otworzył również w Tokio kawiarnię i galerię sztuki BAPE Café, salon fryzjerski BAPE Cuts i sklep dla dzieci BAPE Kids. W Hongkongu sklep BAPE jest otwarty tylko dla osób posiadających członkostwo. W Tajpej kolejka oczekujących na otwarcie nowego butiku BAPE formowała się już poprzedniej nocy i sięgała kilku przecznic. BAPE'owskie Busy Work Shops przeniosły się również do Londynu i Nowego Jorku. W Stanach Zjednoczonych BAPE jest ulubioną marką gwiazd hip-hopu, takich jak Kanye West i Pharrell Williams. Ten ostatni w 2005 roku otworzył z Nigo linię butów Ice Cream oraz markę ubrań o nazwie Billionaire Boys Club, która na wzór BAPE sprzedaje luksusowe ubrania streetowe, m.in. T-shirty, bluzy i czapki w szokująco wysokich cenach.

NOWHERE MAN
Muzyka była pierwszą fascynacją 18-letniego Tomoakiego. Ta miłość szybko przerodziła się w obsesję na punkcie stylowych ubrań. Właśnie wtedy poznał muzykę Run DMC, zaczął nosić jak amerykańscy hiphopowcy Superstars. Mieszkał wówczas z rodzicami na przedmieściu. Po przeprowadzce do Tokio rozpoczął studia w znanej japońskiej szkole mody Bunka Fashion College. W trakcie studiów

FUTU MAGAZINE • This decidedly Dada/Constructivist composition is a blend of El Lissitzky, Kurt Schwitters, and dozens of acolytes during the avant-garde 1920s. **DESIGN FIRM:** Studio8 Design **DESIGNER:** Matt Willey **CLIENT:** *FUTU* magazine **PRIMARY FONTS:** Fat Face, Champion, Chaparral

CONSTRUCTIVIST

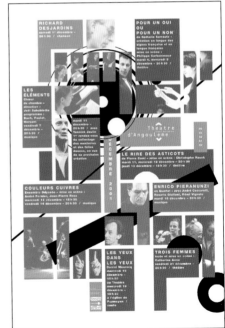

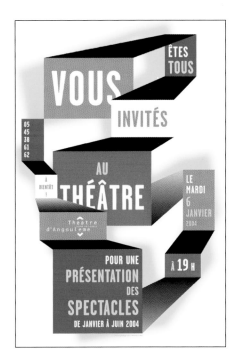

THÉÂTRE D'ANGOULÊME, SEASON POSTERS 2001–2002 • "This series of posters is based on a very classic grid and colour system," says Anette Lenz. "It is the graphic element that allows us to play with the foreground and backround throughout the whole season." **ART DIRECTOR AND DESIGNER:** Anette Lenz **CLIENT:** Théâtre d'Angoulême **PRIMARY FONTS:** Various

CONSTRUCTIVIST

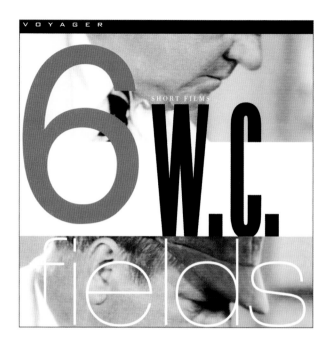

W.C. FIELDS – 6 SHORT FILMS • This advertisement was inspired by film footage and influenced by Paul Rand. "I would never have more than four photos to choose from for a cover," says Terry Koppel, "so the challenge was to make each one fresh and different by integrating bold type and image in a Constructivist layering." **DESIGN FIRM:** T. Koppel Design **ART DIRECTOR AND DESIGNER:** Terry Koppel **CLIENT:** The Criterion Collection **PRIMARY FONTS:** Helvetica Regular, Helvetica Light Extended, Koppel's E17

CHILD'S PLAY • David Wolske was commissioned to design and produce an identity and posters for a series of five lectures by pre-eminent art historians. "I conceived a set of limited-edition letterpress broadsides printed from handset metal and woodtypes," Wolske explains. "This is the fifth poster in the series." Influences include Paul Rand, Bradbury Thompson and Ladislav Sutnar. **ART DIRECTOR, DESIGNER, AND ILLUSTRATOR:** David Wolske **CLIENT:** Indiana University, School of Fine Art, Department of the History of Art **PRIMARY FONTS:** Univers, 19th-century Gothic woodtype

AUSTIN CITY HOMES • Austin City Homes is the dream project of local builder Dan Fawcett. Fascinated and inspired by Eichler Homes from the 1950s and 1960s, he set out to create his own modern mid-century masterpiece in the Texas Hill Country. "The home he built is truly impressive," says Ben Barry, "and we tried to capture both our impression of this house and the mid-century aesthetic when creating his identity system" – with a tip of the hat to Alvin Lustig. **DESIGN FIRM:** The Decoder Ring **DESIGNER:** Ben Barry **CLIENT:** Austin City Homes **PRIMARY FONT:** Soho Gothic

CONSTRUCTIVIST

A LITTLE TOPSEY IN THE TURVEY • This poster for a Book Arts Program workshop led by writer, designer, and book artist Emily McVarish attempts to convey the balance of immediacy and control inherent to her stunning limited-edition book designs. **DESIGNER AND ILLUSTRATOR:** David Wolske **CLIENT:** Book Arts Program, Special Collections, J. Willard Marriott Library, The University of Utah **PRIMARY FONTS:** Knockout, Trade Gothic, Giza

76

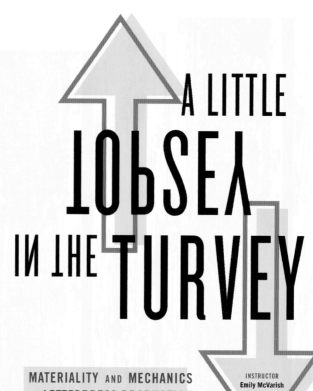

EUROPE 2020 • The inspiration for the text of this mural was one of El Lissitzky's thoughts: "The new book demands new writers." The text of the mural itself reads: "If speech develops in time and writing in space then new times need new writers." Written horizontally, it forms an abstract pattern that symbolizes a melange of languages, cultures, traditions, and religions of European nations. In a sense, it is futuristic and connected with new urban structures. **DESIGN FIRM:** Design Center, Slovenia **DESIGNER:** Eduard Cehovin **PHOTOGRAPHER:** Vojko Kladivar **CLIENT:** IEDC-Bled School of Management, Slovenia **PRIMARY FONT:** Based on Architype Van Doesburg

CONSTRUCTIVIST

LOVE YOUR BIKE • A poster advertising this one-day event, which celebrated bike culture in Portsmouth. The layout for this poster was influenced by modernist pioneers Emil Ruder and Müller-Brockmann. **DESIGN FIRM:** ilovedust **CLIENT:** Love Your Bike Portsmouth **PRIMARY FONTS:** Didot, Nomad, Baskerville

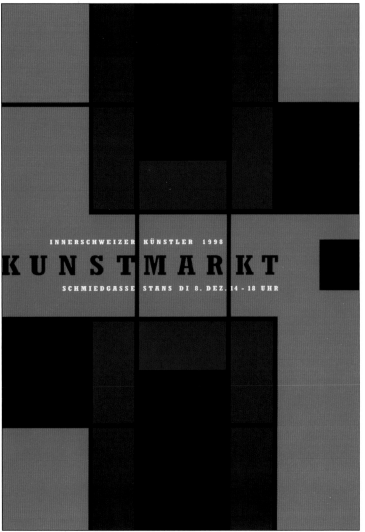

KUNSTMARKT 1998. ARTISTS OF CENTRAL SWITZERLAND, STANS • This announcement for an exhibition of the work of selected artists based in central Switzerland is "a striking interpretation of Russian Constructivism," says Melchior Imboden. **DESIGN FIRM:** Melchior Imboden, Graphic Atelier **ART DIRECTOR AND DESIGNER:** Melchior Imboden **CLIENT:** Gallery Chäslager, Stans **PRIMARY FONT:** Rockwell Bold Condensed

ARTISTS IN EXILE • This book jacket references 1940s Hollywood glamour – how refugees fleeing from the turmoil in 20th-century Europe transformed performing arts in the United States. The red "X" in "exile" brings to mind the aesthetic of the European avant-garde. **DESIGN FIRM:** Archie Ferguson Design **ART DIRECTOR AND DESIGNER:** Archie Ferguson **PUBLISHER:** HarperCollins **PRIMARY FONT:** Gill Sans

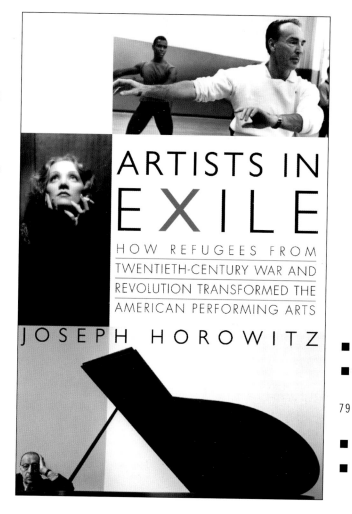

I NEWSPAPER • This is a section-opening spread from *i*, a small-format national Portuguese newspaper. This publication uses a progressive format but "the author of this project, Javier Errea, chose a color and type palette that recalls its newspaper roots," says Nick Mrozowski. The type here was used to emphasize the fact that Portugal's chief prosecutor, whose photograph appears in the bottom-left corner of the page, was then under enormous pressure from more than a few sides. **ART DIRECTOR AND DESIGNER:** Nick Mrozowski **PHOTOGRAPHER:** Pedro Azevedo **CLIENT:** *i* newspaper, Sojormedia Capital **PRIMARY FONT:** Helvetica 75 Bold Condensed

CONSTRUCTIVIST

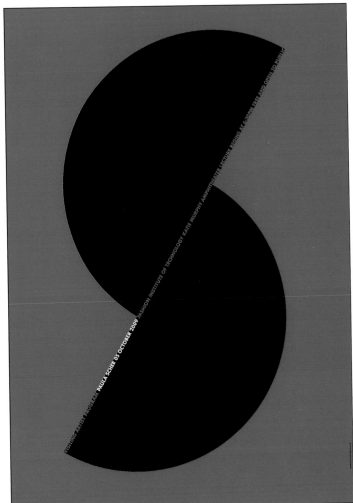

VISITING ARTIST PROGRAM • Rocco Piscatello is a fervent admirer of simplicity, the Swiss/International Style, and Asian Art, which are interestingly blended in these posters. **DESIGN FIRM:** Piscatello Design Centre **DESIGNERS:** Rocco Piscatello, Kimberly Piscatello (Strausfeld Poster) **CLIENT:** Fashion Institute of Technology, New York **PRIMARY FONTS:** Custom P, S, H, D, T, M. Type (experimental) is Akzidenz-Grotesk

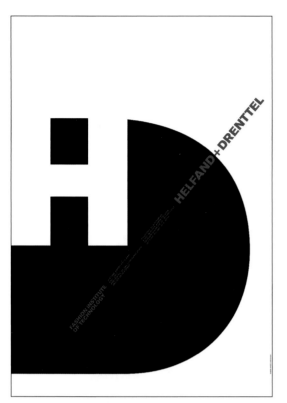

VISITINGARTISTPROGRAM
LISASTRAUSFELD17SEPTE
MBERSTEVENHELLER16OC
TOBERMILTONGLASER13N
OVEMBERALLLECTURESBE
GINAT630PMKATIEMURPH
YAMPHITHEATERFASHION
INSTITUTEOFTECHNOLOGY

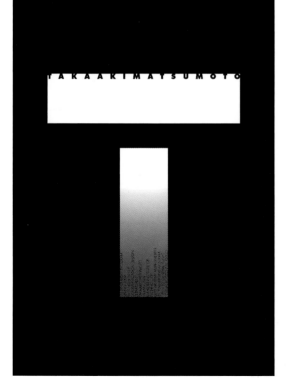

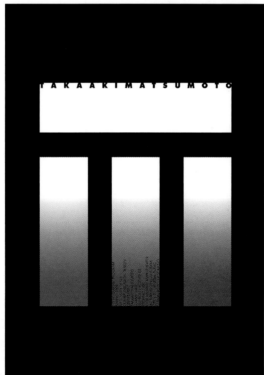

CONSTRUCTIVIST

UN FLAIX AL ROMÀNIC • This kind of pinwheel-style typography requires applying a photography camera diaphragm over different digital color backgrounds (RGB). The poster was designed for the "Un Flaix Al Romànic" (Flash to Romanesque) photography contest organized by the Episcopal Museum of Vic in Barcelona. **DESIGN FIRM:** Bisgrafic **DESIGNER:** Bisgrafic **CLIENT:** MEV (Episcopal Museum of Vic) **PRIMARY FONT:** Helvetica

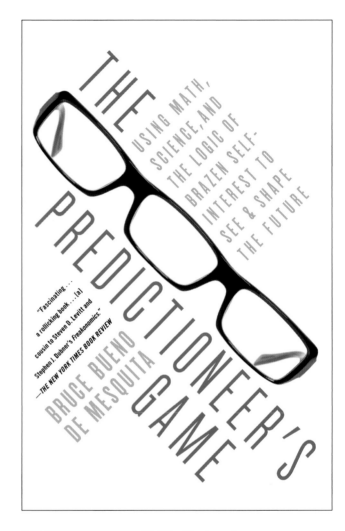

THE PREDICTIONEER'S GAME • The dynamic diagonal, which here frames the three-lens glasses of the "predictioner," is one of the key principles of the Constructivist typographic scheme. **DESIGN FIRM:** De Vicq Design **ART DIRECTOR:** Robbin Schiff **DESIGNER:** Roberto de Vicq de Cumptich **PHOTOGRAPHER:** Tom Schierlitz **PUBLISHER:** Random House **PRIMARY FONT:** Cactus

MAD^2_ONNA

83

MADONNA • While this spread is not strictly a pastiche of Russian Constructivism, it does use some of its characteristics to build tension on the page and between the type and the dramatic photograph. **DESIGN FIRM:** *GQ* **DESIGN DIRECTOR:** Fred Woodward **DESIGNER:** Ken DeLago **CLIENT:** *GQ* **PUBLISHER:** Condé Nast **PRIMARY FONT:** Gotham

CONSTRUCTIVIST

84

LUMPEN MAGAZINE • For over 20 years, *Lumpen* has served as a showcase for outsider opinions on culture, politics, art, and music, all geared towards today's extreme thinker, with a format that borrows tropes from El Lissitzky and other Russian avant-gardists. **DESIGN FIRM:** Plural **ART DIRECTORS AND DESIGNERS:** Jeremiah Chiu, Renata Graw **ILLUSTRATORS:** Andy Burkholder, Jeremiah Chiu, Renata Graw **PHOTOGRAPHERS:** Anticon, Aron Gent, Renata Graw **CLIENT AND PUBLISHER:** Public Media Institute **PRIMARY FONTS:** Custom type, Golden Type, Univers, Bodoni, NE10

BLOC PARTY • For Bloc Party's second tour, designer Dan Stiles introduced the theme of the Communist Bloc, "playing off the famous posters of Lenin pointing the way forward. But since the Soviet Union had fallen apart I introduced the confusion of multiple hands pointing all over the place," he says. **DESIGN FIRM:** Dan Stiles **ART DIRECTOR, DESIGNER, AND ILLUSTRATOR:** Dan Stiles **CLIENT:** Monqui Presents **PRIMARY FONTS:** East Bloc Closed, Blair

ENTANGLEMENT • This work was inspired by the periodic table and Constructivist design. According to Einstein, quantum theory required entanglements – the idea that subatomic particles could become inextricably linked, and that a change to one such particle would instantly be reflected in its counterpart, even if they were separated by a universe. **DESIGN FIRM:** Archie Ferguson Design **ART DIRECTOR AND DESIGNER:** Archie Ferguson **CLIENT:** Four Walls Eight Windows **PRIMARY FONT:** Akzidenz-Grotesk

STENCIL

Although stencil type was developed before the advent of modernism – it was used primarily to label boxes and bags of products such as cotton and tobacco – the modernists adopted the form of the stenciled letter. They did not actually make stencils, but the graphic appeal of the void connective line had a machine-like quality that gave stencil letters an avant-garde look.

86

MAC_06 AND MAC_09 • The 2006 and 2009 editions of this event (organized by the city of Geneva's Cultural Affairs department) offered a journey through contemporary art, animating the city of Geneva with exhibitions, conferences, and tours. The visual identity is defined by its modular typographical composition, which differentiates one event from the next, and the use of Optimo's Cargo font, for its impact. **DESIGN FIRM:** GVA Studio **CLIENT:** Cultural Affairs department, Geneva **PRIMARY FONT:** Cargo

THE GIFTED EYE OF JEAN PLANQUE

A collector's intimacy
Béatrice Delapraz

THE GIFTED EYE OF JEAN PLANQUE • *"The Gifted Eye..."* is a life story drawn from interviews with Planque, an unusual art collector with no formal art education. He became, by accident, an advisor for Fondation Beyeler (one of the greatest European galleries) and the friend of many famous painters (Picasso, Dubuffet, Léger, and others). His own collection, hidden in his rustic house and protected by no insurance or alarm system, included hundreds of pieces by the great 20th-century masters. To reflect Planque's rough and simple character, Pesce drew a typeface inspired by Fernand Léger's books and lettering. **DESIGN FIRM:** Atelier Poisson **ART DIRECTOR, DESIGNER, AND ILLUSTRATOR:** Giorgio Pesce **CLIENT:** Béatrice Delapraz **PUBLISHER:** Editions Cheneau-de-Bourg **PRIMARY FONTS:** Hand-drawn, Clarendon

87

STENCIL

AMIRAL FONT SPECIMEN • This
font was inspired by lettering on boats
and containers. Amiral is a dark stencil
typeface, used only in uppercases with
alternate figures. **DESIGN FIRM:** Bureau
205 **ART DIRECTOR:** Damien Gautier
DESIGNERS: Damien Gautier, Quentin
Margat **CLIENT AND PUBLISHER:** Editions
205 **PRIMARY FONT:** Amiral

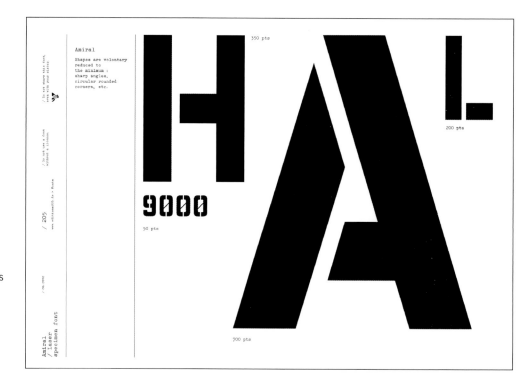

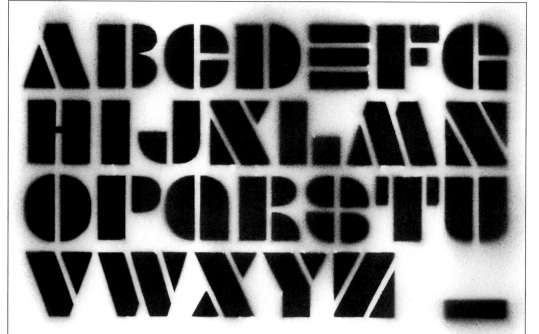

AIGA TOMATO TALK • This dirty
stencil harkens back to the everyday
usage of the typeface as a means
of identifying packages and bales.
DESIGN FIRM: Tomato **DESIGNER:**
Dylan Kendle **ILLUSTRATOR:** Julie
Verhoeven **CLIENT:** AIGA **PRIMARY
FONT:** USAAF Stencil

GEORGE CLOONEY AND RENÉE ZELLWEGER • Lower-case stencil customized with a Bauhaus-inspired simplicity and used in a minimalist way for this magazine photo spread. **DESIGN FIRM:** *W* Magazine **ART DIRECTOR AND DESIGNER:** Nathalie Kirsheh **PHOTOGRAPHER:** Michael Thompson **PUBLISHER:** Condé Nast **PRIMARY FONT:** Illustrated type

AVEC – the font in 3 weights

Praline 2010

AVEC • Invited to take part in a group exhibition called "If You Could Collaborate," the aim of which was to provide a platform for the finest creatives from all over the world to question their conventional working methods and trigger unusual collaborations, the graphic designers at Praline thought of Mike Fairbrass from the RSHP Model Shop as the ideal partner. Together they have created a new font called AVEC, which is based on architectural floor-plans. It exists in three weights: Floorplay, Mezzanine, and Facade. **ART DIRECTORS:** Praline, Mike Fairbrass **DESIGNERS:** David Tanguy, Mike Fairbrass, Nina Klein **PHOTOGRAPHER:** Mike Fairbrass **PUBLISHER:** If You Could **PRIMARY FONT:** AVEC

STENCIL

COSTA NAVARINO FONT • Praline created this bespoke font, Costa Sans, for a Greek developer. The font is based on the Greek Linear B syllabary, which pre-dates the Greek alphabet. The simple and geometric letters also reference modernist typefaces such as Futura. The result is an uncomplicated, contemporary alphabet. It comes in two weights: Regular and Bold. A special stencil version has been designed for wayfinding signage. **DESIGN FIRM:** Praline (in collaboration with Less Rain) **ART DIRECTOR:** David Tanguy **DESIGNERS:** David Tanguy, Rob Peart **CLIENT:** T.E.MES S.A. Costa Navarino **PRIMARY FONT:** Costa Sans

COSTA FONT

REGULAR
ABCDEFGHIJKLMNOPQRSTUVWXYZ
1234567890

BOLD
ABCDEFGHIJKLMNOPQRSTUVWXYZ
1234567890

STENCIL
ABCDEFGHIJKLMNOPQRSTUVWXYZ
1234567890

90

UPRISING • This handlettering, designed for a fashion editorial spread, adds both a handmade quality and a monumental touch to the page. **DESIGN FIRM:** Faith **ART DIRECTOR AND DESIGNER:** Paul Sych **PHOTOGRAPHER:** Greg Sorensen **PUBLISHER:** *Lush* magazine **PRIMARY FONT:** Custom

AIGA TOMATO TALK • In this poster design the layers of stencils have a feel that is both vintage and contemporary. **DESIGN FIRM:** Tomato **DESIGNER:** Dylan Kendle **CLIENT:** AIGA **PRIMARY FONT:** Reworked USAAF Stencil

LANDESMUSEUM ZÜRICH • The combination of armored knights and contemporary type adds to the drama of this image. **DESIGN FIRM:** L2M3 Kommunikationsdesign GmbH **ART DIRECTOR:** Sascha Lobe **DESIGNERS:** Sascha Lobe, Oliver Wörle **PHOTOGRAPHER:** Florian Hammerich **CLIENT:** Landesmuseum Zürich **PRIMARY FONTS:** Cargo, Akkurat

STENCIL

US TODAY AFTER • This poster for the Photography Biennale in Lyon, France, uses a lettering based on stencil fonts. **ART DIRECTORS:** Damien Gautier, Quentin Margat **DESIGNERS:** Damien Gautier, Quentin Margat **PHOTOGRAPHER:** Andrew Bush **CLIENT:** Septembre de la Photographie, Lyon **PUBLISHER:** Editions 205 **PRIMARY FONTS:** Colonel, Robin, Pica 10 Pitch

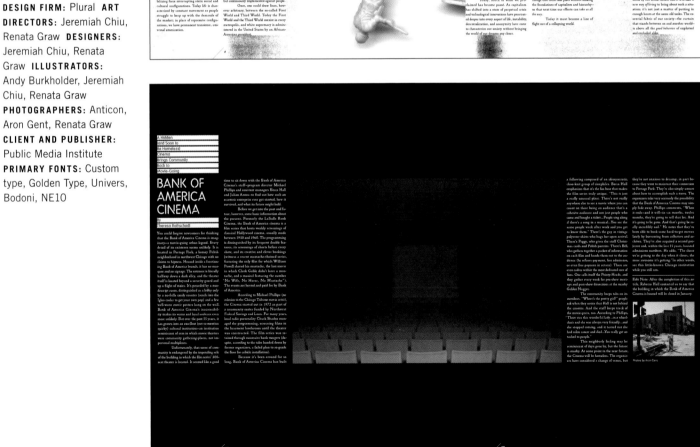

LUMPEN MAGAZINE •
Another example of Plural's design work for the iconic *Lumpen* magazine.
DESIGN FIRM: Plural **ART DIRECTORS:** Jeremiah Chiu, Renata Graw **DESIGNERS:** Jeremiah Chiu, Renata Graw **ILLUSTRATORS:** Andy Burkholder, Jeremiah Chiu, Renata Graw **PHOTOGRAPHERS:** Anticon, Aron Gent, Renata Graw **CLIENT AND PUBLISHER:** Public Media Institute **PRIMARY FONTS:** Custom type, Golden Type, Univers, Bodoni, NE10

STENCIL

POBEDA • Praline chose to use the Glaser Stencil font for its directness and simplicity. It echoed the refurbished industrial building in which the gallery opened and could be actually stenciled on the walls and die-cut on invitations and other printed materials. The Cyrillic characters follow the drawings of the original font and the cut lines are adapted to the Russian characters. "It was important to keep the same feel and to make sure the new letters would feel as if they were part of the Glaser family," says Tanguy. "It was especially interesting for us to design such type as none of us speaks Russian." **DESIGN FIRM:** Praline **ART DIRECTOR:** David Tanguy **DESIGNERS:** Al Rodger, David Tanguy **CLIENT:** POBEDA Gallery, Moscow **PRIMARY FONT:** Glaser Stencil

94

INSECURITY • Every month, Italian magazine *Domus* features a themed 24-page "intersection." In this design for the March 2008 edition, the theme, insecurity, is counterbalanced by the typographic authority. **DESIGN FIRM:** Tomato **ART DIRECTORS:** John Warwicker, Simon Taylor **DESIGNER:** John Warwicker **CLIENT:** *Domus* Magazine, Italy **PUBLISHER:** *Domus* magazine **PRIMARY FONTS:** Cargo, Lubalin Graph, Dot Matrix

PLAYFUL

THANKS IN LARGE PART to the projected austerity and simplicity of postwar Swiss design, modern was stereotyped as cold and unforgiving. If the leading or the point size was just a fraction off the assigned grid, then fire and brimstone would await. In this stereotypical profile there is no room for error or divergence. However, most stereotypes are exaggerations. And so it is for modern type and typography as far as the cliché of "cold and unforgiving" goes.

Less is more, much of the time. But the belief that any form of play is absent from this equation is false. As Paul Rand stated, modernism is a set of philosophical – and even spiritual – dictates. But unlike the ethos of the late 19th- and early 20th-century Shakers, for whom "less is more" was a rigid religious doctrine, the dictums of modernism are a means of achieving balance and obtaining freedom from the tyranny of fashion.

Play is an essential part of modern design and a key characteristic of modernist typography. Rand called his sense of abandon the "Play Principle:" a license to push away from the grid and from all the fundamental design rules.

When the Swiss devised strict rules against using more than one or two typefaces moored to specific matrices, it was to put an end – if only briefly – to the chaos that reigned in design at the time. But the rigid approach had a limited shelf life and soon became stale. Even the leading Swiss graphic designers, such as Armin Hofmann and Josef Müller-Brockmann, saw the need (and felt the desire) to be more playful, to distort, contrast, and exaggerate design components for graphic impact and mnemonic effect.

This section focuses on the work of new modern typographers who build concepts around the ability playfully to invent alternatives and break rules. By employing computer techniques never available to the "vintage moderns," contemporary designers can toy with type and extend the boundaries and definition of "modern."

WIT, HUMOR, AND TRANSFORMATION

COMIC

Modernism was not known for its humorous approaches to type and layout, but nonetheless a subtle wit pervaded much of modernism's leading design sensibilities. The neomoderns often use simplicity and economy as a foil for satire. Comic design does not have to be comic strip or slapstick. The examples shown here integrate modern design principles with winks and nods.

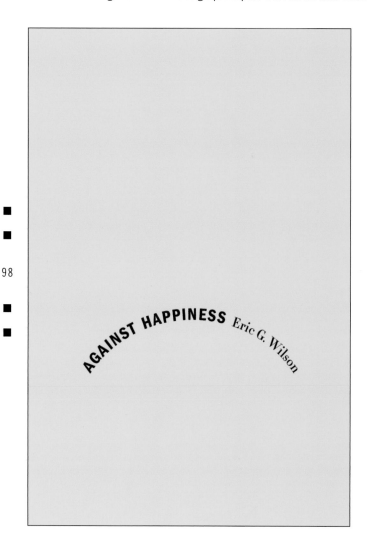

AGAINST HAPPINESS • A classic yellow smiley face is an obvious nod to contemporary popular culture. "Americans are obsessed with happiness," says Jennifer Carrow, "but who says we're supposed to be happy? Eric G. Wilson argues that melancholia is a necessary part of any thriving culture, that it is the muse of great literature, painting, music, and innovation." **ART DIRECTOR:** Susan Mitchell **DESIGNER:** Jennifer Carrow **CLIENT:** Sarah Crichton Books/Farrar, Straus and Giroux **PRIMARY FONTS:** Franklin Gothic, Didot

BLOC PARTY • What could be more modern and anti-modern at the same time than Mao? The type here, however, is Soviet-inspired. The Chinese and the Soviets, history tells us, did not get along. **DESIGN FIRM:** Dan Stiles **ART DIRECTOR, DESIGNER, AND ILLUSTRATOR:** Dan Stiles **CLIENT:** Monqui Presents **PRIMARY FONT:** East Bloc Closed

HARRAH'S ENTERTAINMENT EMPLOYEE REWARDS CAMPAIGN • WPA posters and travel posters publicized this employee engagement campaign. Typically, this kind of campaign falls within the domain of HR specialists and involves little more than shotgun emails. Harrah's Entertainment, the world's largest casino entertainment company, had bigger ideas. They wanted to launch a new customer service rewards program for their 25,000 employees, who work in 35 different sites. They wanted to excite, engage, and invigorate their team. Harrah's turned to Hatch for help with virtually every aspect of the integrated communications campaign. Hatch not only named the program – "Total Service, Total Rewards" – but they created posters, a website, direct mail, table toppers, self-service kiosks, and even a "Price is Right" game show idea to help managers introduce the new program. **DESIGN FIRM:** Hatch Design **ART DIRECTORS:** Katie Jain, Joel Templin **DESIGNER AND ILLUSTRATOR:** Ryan Meis **CLIENT:** Harrah's Entertainment **PRIMARY FONT:** Knockout

COMIC

CAN THEY DO THAT? • "This was another killed book cover proposal," laments Matt Dorfman, "for a book written by someone in the American Civil Liberties Union that explored the myriad ways in which office workers' civil liberties are regularly infringed upon by the corporations they work for." The references, he adds, are "paper shredders and unspoken, interpersonal office formalities."
DESIGN FIRM: Matt Dorfman/Metalmother
ART DIRECTOR: Joseph Perez **DESIGNER:** Matt Dorfman **CLIENT:** Portfolio Books (Penguin)
PRIMARY FONT: Akzidenz-Grotesk (Berthold)

OUR DAILY MEDS • Catherine Casalino wanted to address the issue of the commercialism of the pharmaceutical industry and came up with a Warhol-style illustration of prescription bottles. To push the idea further, the title panel was made to look like the label of a prescription bottle. "Warhol's soup cans were the inspiration," says the designer.
DESIGN FIRM: Catherine Casalino Design **ART DIRECTOR:** Henry Sene Yee **DESIGNER AND ILLUSTRATOR:** Catherine Casalino **CLIENT:** Picador Books **PRIMARY FONT:** Helvetica

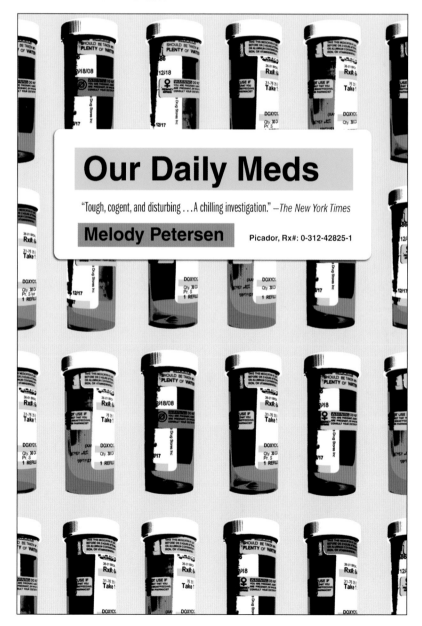

the g●od enuf rvlutn

FROM DIGITAL MUSIC TO VIDEO CAMERAS TO MILITARY AIRCRAFT, CHEAP AND SIMPLE BEATS PERFECT ALMOST EVERY TIME. IT'S CALLED THE MP3 EFFECT, AND IT WILL CHANGE EVERYTHING.

Why lo-fi high tech will rule the world.

BY ROBERT CAPPS

IN 2001, JONATHAN KAPLAN AND ARIEL Braunstein noticed a quirk in the camera market. All the growth was in expensive digital cameras, but the best-selling units by far were still cheap, disposable film models. That year, a whopping 181 million disposables were sold in the US, compared with around 7 million digital cameras. Spotting an opportunity, Kaplan and Braunstein formed a company called Pure Digital Technologies and set out to see if they could mix the rich chocolate of digital imaging with the mass-market peanut butter of throwaway point-and-shoots. They called their brainchild the Single Use Digital Camera and cobranded it with retailers, mostly pharmacies like CVS. ¶ The concept looked promising, but it turned out to be fatally flawed. The problem, says Simon Fleming-Wood, a member of Pure Digital's founding management

PHOTOGRAPHS BY KENJI AOKI

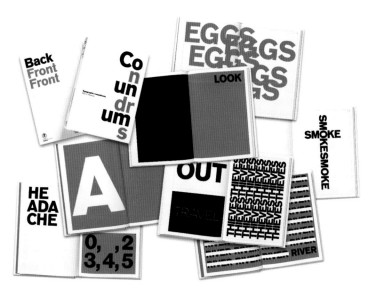

THE GOOD ENOUGH REVOLUTION • This simple page of type looks like it came right out of a Futura specimen sheet, and yet it also has a totally contemporary aesthetic. **DESIGN FIRM:** *Wired* magazine **DESIGN DIRECTOR:** Wyatt Mitchell **CREATIVE DIRECTOR:** Scott Dadich **DESIGNERS:** Maili Holiman, Scott Dadich **PHOTOGRAPHER:** Kenji Aoki **PUBLISHER:** Condé Nast **PRIMARY FONT:** Futura

CONUNDRUMS • The timeless modern classic sensibility of this design is neutral and overt. The pages focus the eye on the message without a hint of ambiguity – but with considerable wit. **DESIGN FIRM:** Pentagram Design **DESIGNER:** Harry Pearce **PHOTOGRAPHER:** Nick Turner **CLIENT:** HarperCollins **PRIMARY FONT:** AG Old Face

COMIC

BOOKA SHADE – REGENERATE/REMIX COVER •
For Booka Shade's fourth album and its accompanying singles and promotional material, "We used the font we had designed in 2004 to construct the Booka Shade logo, and set the information straight," says design firm Hort. The designer's influences include Robert Indiana's LOVE sculpture, basic Bauhaus shapes, and posters for both the 1923 Bauhaus exhibition in Weimar (by Rudolf Baschant) and the '50 Years of Bauhaus' exhibition (by Herbert Bayer). **DESIGN FIRM:** Hort **ART DIRECTOR AND DESIGNER:** Hort **CLIENT:** Get Physical Music **PRIMARY FONTS:** Selfmade, Akzidenz-Grotesk

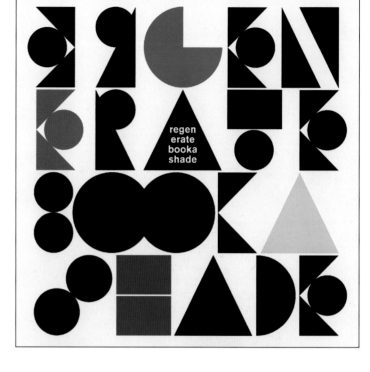

> JOURNEY TO THE
(REVOLUTIONARY, EVIL-HATING, CASH-CRAZY, AND POSSIBLY SELF-DESTRUCTIVE)
CENTER OF

$G00,000,000,000,00
0,000,000,000,000,00
000,000,000,000,000
0,000,000,000,000,00
000,000,000,000,000
0,000,000,000,GLE.00

> You've heard the story. **Larry and Sergey**
drop out of school, start a company in a garage,
refuse to play nice with **Silicon Valley**, then
become billionaires by defying Wall Street. >

260.00.03.05

> The problem is, it leaves out the most
important chapter—the mystery
about whether **Larry and Sergey**
will actually grow up **by John Heilemann** >

G00,000,GLE • This design for magazine *GQ* is not only totally contemporary, it is also a hilarious way of creating a title that illustrates the article's story: Google's accumulation of wealth requires that many zeros. **DESIGN DIRECTOR:** Fred Woodward **DESIGNER:** Ken DeLago **CLIENT:** *GQ* **PUBLISHER:** Condé Nast **PRIMARY FONT:** Titling

GAY MALE PORNOGRAPHY •
Pornography is overt, so the visual
pun of the "A" as an erection is not
really pornography. Rather, it is the
suggestion of something naughty –
and funny. **DESIGN FIRM:** Salamander
Hill Design **DESIGNER:** David
Drummond **CLIENT:** Rachel Moeller
PUBLISHER: University of Minnesota
Press **PRIMARY FONTS:** Trade Gothic,
New Baskerville

MORI ART MUSEUM • The humorous typographic treatments add visual appeal to these multilingual designs for one of Tokyo's leading contemporary art museums. **DESIGN FIRM:** Barnbrook **ART DIRECTOR:** Jonathan Barnbrook **DESIGNERS:** Jonathan Barnbrook, Marcus Leis Allion, Pedro Inoue **CLIENT:** Mori Art Museum **PRIMARY FONT:** Bourgeois

RUNAWAY BRANDS

TEXT — HELENA CHMIELEWSKA-SZLAJFER

Marka, której wizerunek wymknął się odgórnym ustaleniom specjalistów, to spełnienie najgorszych marketingowych snów. Co więcej, przytrafiło się to niejednej z tych o zbyt wielkim, jak się okazało, apetycie na masowy rynek A brand image that has escaped the control of specialists is marketing's worst nightmare. What's more, it has happened to more than one brand with too big of an appetite for the market

132

133

FUTU MAGAZINE • For this bilingual article, Matt Willey has used typography in an expressive way. On this spread, the type itself rather overtly runs away into the horizon. **DESIGN FIRM:** Studio8 Design **DESIGNER:** Matt Willey **CLIENT:** *FUTU* magazine **PRIMARY FONTS:** Fat Face, Champion, Chaparral

"A landmark of environmental reporting. . . . A preview of chemical horrors yet to come . . . takes up where *Silent Spring* left off."
—STEWART L. UDALL, former U. S. Secretary of the Interior

THE POISONING OF

Michigan

Joyce Egginton

Afterword by Devra Lee Davis, Maryann Donovan, and Arlene Blum

THE POISONING OF MICHIGAN • Understatement and upside-down statements work hand-in-hand here. The typography is fettered, allowing the upside-down twist to be the focal point. "Michigan" on its back evokes the topic of the book better than any illustration could. **DESIGN FIRM:** Salamander Hill Design **DESIGNER:** David Drummond **CLIENT:** Annette Tanner **PUBLISHER:** University of Michigan Press **PRIMARY FONTS:** Trade Gothic, New Baskerville

COMIC

THE ART OF LIVING

MEL THOMPSON

ME • The simplicity of this typographical concept is its strength. The artlessness of the design gives the rather basic topic – "me" – depth and impact. **DESIGN FIRM:** Salamander Hill Design **DESIGNER:** David Drummond **CLIENT:** Neil de Cort **PUBLISHER:** Polity Press **PRIMARY FONT:** Futura

FIELD'S SWEET SPOT • Clearly, 1960s Mod fashions, patterns, and vintage candy packaging are the underpinnings of this witty design. This particular candy was destined to be stocked in a famous department store. **DESIGN FIRM:** Wink **ART DIRECTORS:** Richard Boynton, Scott Thares **DESIGNER AND ILLUSTRATOR:** Richard Boynton **CLIENT:** Marshall Field's **PRIMARY FONTS:** Chalet, Futura, Helvetica Condensed, Helvetica Extended

ALAN GREENSPAN TAKES A BATH • As chairman of the U.S. Federal Reserve, Alan Greenspan had the power to influence the health of the financial markets. The typography suggests his entanglement with Wall Street and the world of finance. **DESIGN DIRECTOR:** Fred Woodward **DESIGNER:** Ken DeLago **CLIENT:** *GQ* **PUBLISHER:** Condé Nast **PRIMARY FONT:** Sentinel

$+A\frac{1}{4}n$ $Gr\frac{3}{3}n$- ...span $Tak\frac{3}{5}$... a Bath

GQ + 209 ●●●

For the past eighteen years, the Oz-like ALAN GREENSPAN has used his position as chairman of the Federal Reserve to push, behind the scenes, for strict budgetary discipline. Now, in his final year in office, he has watched the Bush administration destroy the budget surplus and drive the deficit to record highs. So the mysterious chairman must decide: Will he continue to fight for his economic principles, even if it means fighting his own party? by WIL S. HYLTON

●●● Illustration by NOLI NOVAK

COMIC

JAQK CELLARS • For the creation of this brand, which combines wine and gaming, design firm Hatch named the company, as well as each wine, and came up with a tag line: "Play a Little." They did all the design work and sourced every single material, going as far as finding a specialist glass boutique in Milan to create a customized bottle for JAQK's flagship Cabernet. **DESIGN FIRM:** Hatch Design **ART DIRECTORS:** Katie Jain, Joel Templin **DESIGNERS:** Eszter T. Clark, Ryan Meis **CLIENT:** JAQK Cellars **PRIMARY FONTS:** Clarendon, Gotham

DR. DELICIOUS • Featuring a book on a book cover is not a new idea – but this is probably the first time that the idea of presenting a book on the cover of a book as a tasty morsel has been cooked up. **DESIGN FIRM:** Salamander Hill Design **DESIGNER:** David Drummond **CLIENT:** Simon Dardick **PUBLISHER:** Vehicule Press **PRIMARY FONTS:** Trade Gothic, Futura

HNW, INC. IS THE FIRST AND ONLY INTEGRATED MARKETING SERVICES FIRM THAT FOCUSES EXCLUSIVELY ON STRATEGY AND COMMUNICATIONS IN THE HIGH-NET WORTH MARKET. SINCE OUR FOUNDING IN 1999, HNW HAS PROVIDED A UNIQUE BLEND OF CONSULTING AND CREATIVE SERVICES, FROM STRATEGY TO EXECUTION. OUR VIEW OF WEALTH MANAGEMENT IS HOLISTIC, EMPHASIZING INVESTMENTS, LIFESTYLE AND PHILANTHROPY.

OUR MISSION IS TO HELP FINANCIAL SERVICES INSTITUTIONS AND LUXURY MARKETERS UNDERSTAND, ACQUIRE AND RETAIN INDIVIDUALS WITHIN THE HIGH-NET WORTH SEGMENT.

HNW, INC. • This self-promotion piece for a marketing agency features timeless yet contemporary typography, with a humorous illustration. **DESIGN FIRM:** HNW, Inc. **ART DIRECTOR AND DESIGNER:** Terry Koppel **PHOTOGRAPHER:** Manipulated photograph **CLIENT AND PUBLISHER:** HNW, Inc. **PRIMARY FONTS:** Didot L96, Didot M16

DAVOR VRANKIĆ • The choice of a monochromatic pattern for this catalog cover design was determined by the many monochromatic patterns in Vrankić's own pieces. Milton Glaser's Baby Teeth font was used for the "D" and "V" letters that are made to look like the eyes of a mask. They allow the viewer to catch a glimpse of part of the image inside the book. As the artist, Vrankić, is Croatian, the designer has chosen Typonine Sans, created by a well-known Croatian type designer, as the main body type. **DESIGN FIRM:** Mirko Ilić Corp. **ART DIRECTOR:** Mirko Ilić **DESIGNERS:** Jee-eun Lee, Mirko Ilić **CLIENT:** Galerija likovnih umjetnosti, Osijek **PRIMARY FONTS:** Baby Teeth, Typonine Sans Pro

DAVOR VRANKIĆ
DOZVOLI DA TE UČINIM STVARNIM • LET ME MAKE YOU REAL

COMIC

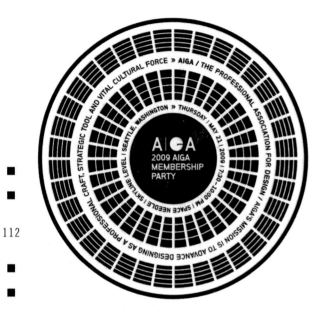

2009 AIGA SEATTLE INVITATION • The Seattle chapter of the American Institute of Graphic Arts (AIGA) asked Turnstyle to design invitations for their 2009 membership party. The only stipulation was that the design should highlight the venue: the Space Needle, Seattle's famous observation tower. "We knew that the last thing any designer in Seattle would want to see was yet another cliché photo or icon of the Space Needle," says Steven Watson. "We abstracted the 'AIGA' letterforms so they could be cut out and assembled into a three-dimensional paper model of the Space Needle, with details about the party on the saucer. It was serendipitous that the letters A-I-G-A could be reconfigured into an approximation of the Space Needle. If this had been an invitation for the YMCA, it wouldn't have worked." **DESIGN FIRM:** Turnstyle **ART DIRECTOR AND DESIGNER:** Steven Watson **CLIENT:** AIGA Seattle **PRIMARY FONT:** Neubau Grotesk

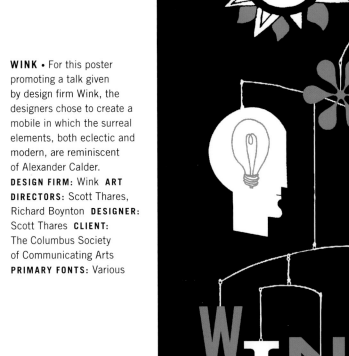

WINK • For this poster promoting a talk given by design firm Wink, the designers chose to create a mobile in which the surreal elements, both eclectic and modern, are reminiscent of Alexander Calder.
DESIGN FIRM: Wink **ART DIRECTORS:** Scott Thares, Richard Boynton **DESIGNER:** Scott Thares **CLIENT:** The Columbus Society of Communicating Arts **PRIMARY FONTS:** Various

113

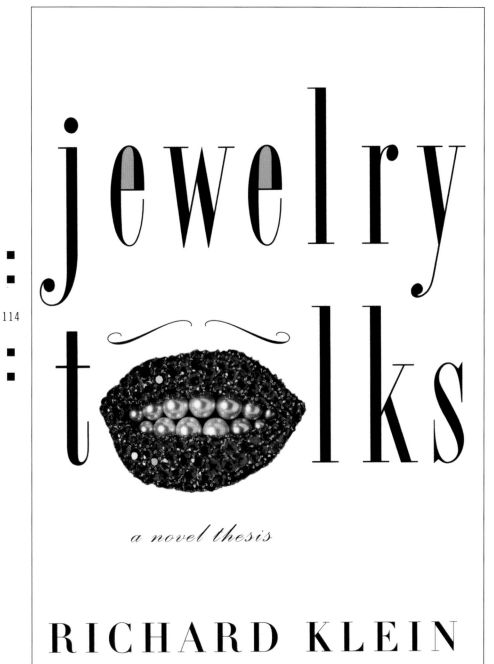

JEWELRY TALKS • In this funny book that is part-novel and part-thesis on jewelry, the narrator is a cross-dresser. Salvador Dalí's *Ruby Lips* topped by the artist's famous mustache directly evoke all these themes. **DESIGN FIRM:** Archie Ferguson Design **ART DIRECTOR AND DESIGNER:** Archie Ferguson **ILLUSTRATOR:** *Ruby Lips* by Salvador Dalí, 1949 **PUBLISHER:** Pantheon Books **PRIMARY FONT:** Custom

DAUB & BAUBLE • The primary influences for this promotional material for a line of hand soaps and creams were 1960s point-of-purchase posters. **DESIGN FIRM:** Wink **ART DIRECTORS:** Richard Boynton, Scott Thares **DESIGNER AND ILLUSTRATOR:** Richard Boynton **CLIENT:** Daub & Bauble **PRIMARY FONTS:** New Century Schoolbook, Trade Gothic Extended, Handlettering

№ 003

Daub&Bauble®

TAROCCO ORANGE AND CLOVE

COMIC

HONEY & MACKIE'S • Honey & Mackie's is an ice cream shop for kids that caters to parents. The name of the company comes from the nicknames of the owners' children, and the ingredients in these ice creams are all natural, organic, and locally grown. As a result, the branding and packaging needed to be modern, authentic, and fun for kids. The carnival type says it all. **DESIGN FIRM:** Wink **ART DIRECTORS:** Scott Thares, Richard Boynton **DESIGNER AND ILLUSTRATOR:** Scott Thares **PHOTOGRAPHER:** Rat Race Studios **CLIENT:** Honey & Mackie's **PRIMARY FONTS:** Futura, Cooper, Cottonwood, Banana Split, Garamond, Trade Gothic, handlettering.

116

HOCUS POTUS • In this design for a book cover, the type acts as grounding for the satiric artwork that shows George W. Bush holding a bomb as though it were an atomic phallus. **DESIGN FIRM:** Kelly Blair Design **DESIGNER AND PHOTOGRAPHER:** Kelly Blair **PUBLISHER:** Melville House Publishing **PRIMARY FONT:** Franklin Gothic

PUNK ROCK VS SWISS MODERNISM • For the poster advertising their talk at the Minneapolis College of Art and Design (MCAD) on the subject of "Punk Rock vs Swiss Modernism," Post Typography decided to "bring these two movements together." They decided to turn an Helvetica "t" upside down "because nothing says 'punk' like an inverted cross." **DESIGN FIRM:** Post Typography **ART DIRECTORS AND DESIGNERS:** Nolen Strals, Bruce Willen **CLIENT:** Minneapolis College of Art and Design **PRIMARY FONT:** Helvetica

COMIC

ADAM & EVE • The Bifur typeface designed by A.M. Cassandre was particularly adapted for this project: the design of a special box that brings together the forestudy and the etching of Rembrandt's *Adam and Eve* (1638). Bifur is used both on the carry case and on the accompanying poster. The case's straps are incorporated into the design, as is the wooden texture of the box. **DESIGN FIRM:** Niessen & de Vries **ART DIRECTORS AND DESIGNERS:** Richard Niessen, Esther de Vries **CLIENT:** Prentenkabinet Leiden **PRIMARY FONTS:** Bifur, Peignot

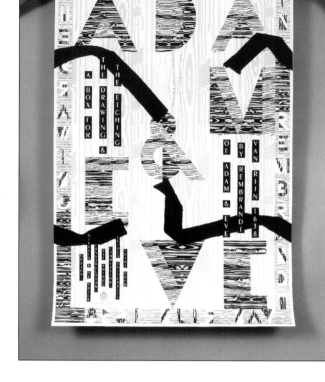

CHEESE CULTURE • Cheese Culture is a new cheese wholesaler that supplies Australian restaurants, importing the finest cheeses from around the world. The identity developed for this brand was inspired by the trademarks most artisan cheesemakers press into their products. **DESIGN FIRM:** Parallax Design **DESIGNER:** Kellie Campbell-Illingworth **CLIENT:** Cheese Culture **PRIMARY FONTS:** Handlettered, Galaxie Polaris

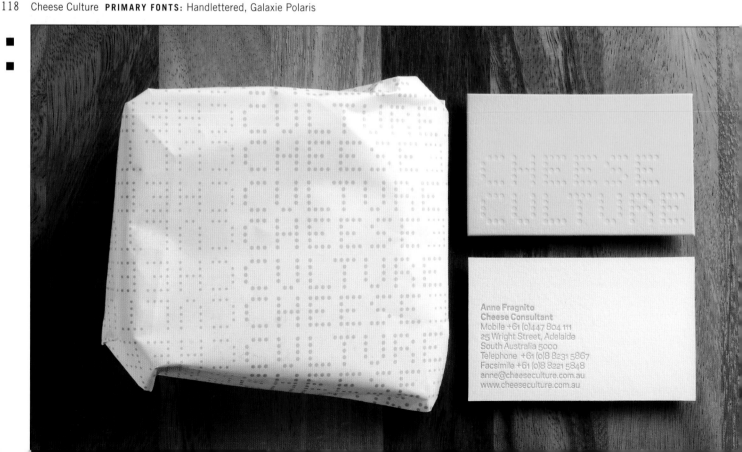

Anne Fragnito
Cheese Consultant
Mobile +61 (0)447 804 111
25 Wright Street, Adelaide
South Australia 5000
Telephone +61 (0)8 8231 5867
Facsimile +61 (0)8 8221 5848
anne@cheeseculture.com.au
www.cheeseculture.com.au

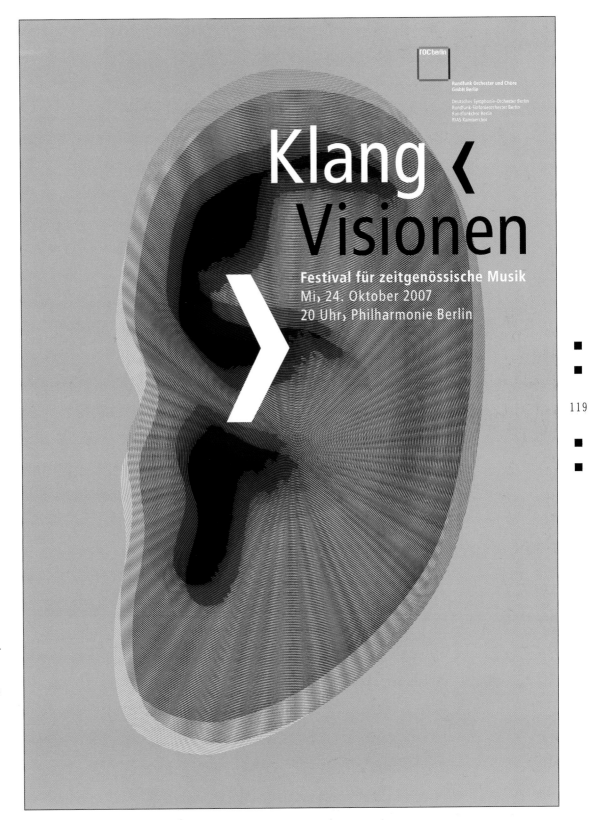

Klang ‹
Visionen

Festival für zeitgenössische Musik
Mi, 24. Oktober 2007
20 Uhr, Philharmonie Berlin

ROCberlin

Rundfunk Orchester und Chöre
GmbH Berlin

Deutsches Symphonie-Orchester Berlin
Rundfunk-Sinfonieorchester Berlin
Rundfunkchor Berlin
RIAS Kammerchor

SOUND VISIONS (KLANG VISIONEN) • This is a poster and corporate design for ROC Berlin, an organization that is composed of the city's four largest orchestras and choirs. The vibrating ear speaks to the incredible volume of the music. **DESIGN FIRM:** Fons Hickmann m23 **ART DIRECTOR:** Fons Hickmann **DESIGNER:** Thomas Schrott **CLIENT:** ROC Berlin **PRIMARY FONT:** Transit

COMIC

TOEVAL GEZOCHT BOOK • The letters forming 'Toeval Gezocht' are made up of lines that are drawn by hand but these letters also seem to fall apart, scattered over the pages as if they were Mikado sticks lying in accidental formations. The positions of these lines play various roles. For instance, they form page-borders in the layout of articles and were animated for a dvd and the Toeval Gezocht website. **DESIGN FIRM:** Niessen & de Vries **ART DIRECTORS AND DESIGNERS:** Richard Niessen, Esther de Vries **CLIENT:** Stichting Toeval Gezocht **PUBLISHER:** Lemniscaat **PRIMARY FONTS:** Toeval Gezocht font (created by the designers), Akzidenz-Grotesk, Didot

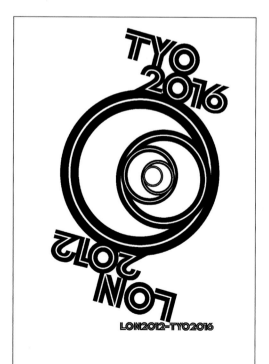

LONDON 2012–TOKYO 2016 • Athletics and arena sports markings designed to promote Tokyo's 2016 Olympic bid. **DESIGN FIRM:** Tomato **DESIGNER:** Simon Taylor **CLIENT:** Nano Universe **PRIMARY FONT:** Hand-drawn

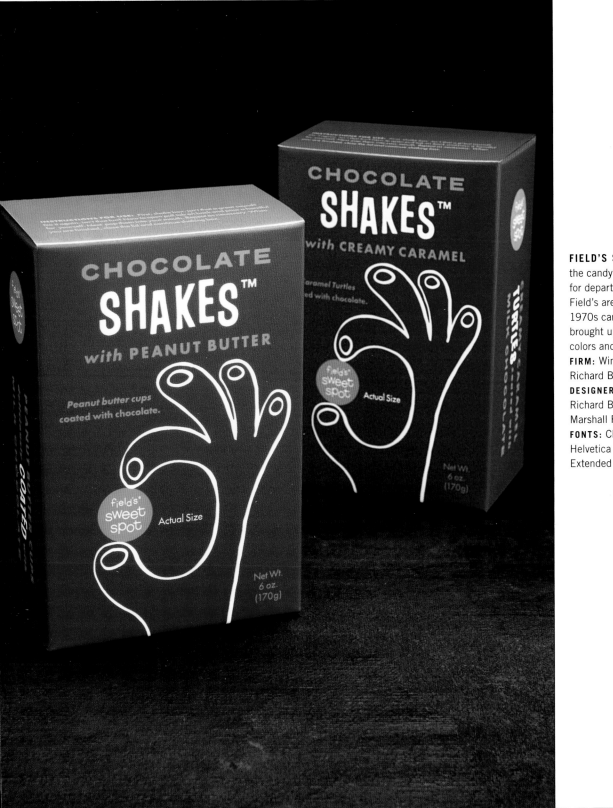

FIELD'S SWEET SPOT • All the candy packages created for department store Marshall Field's are imbued with a 1970s cartoon aesthetic, brought up to date through colors and illustration. **DESIGN FIRM:** Wink **ART DIRECTORS:** Richard Boynton, Scott Thares **DESIGNER AND ILLUSTRATOR:** Richard Boynton **CLIENT:** Marshall Field's **PRIMARY FONTS:** Chalet, Futura, Helvetica Condensed, Helvetica Extended

DECORATIVE

Modernism prided itself on rejecting the decorative tendencies of art nouveau and other bourgeois styles. But art moderne (or art deco) married decorative approaches with a sense of contemporary functionality. These examples embrace both the modern spirit and a passion for the ornamental.

ROCK THE SUIT • The modernist conceit is to avoid ornament but modern ornament does exist, although it is nuanced. The decorative touch of the "o" in "Rock" is based on "page proofs," Woodward says. **DESIGN DIRECTOR:** Fred Woodward **DESIGNER:** Thomas Alberty **PHOTOGRAPHER:** Richard Burbridge **CLIENT:** *GQ* **PUBLISHER:** Condé Nast **PRIMARY FONT:** Futura

122

let every star shine

When YOU shop at MACY'S, you SUPPORT causes in EXTRAORDINARY ways. From EDUCATION and ART'S programs to HEALTH research and SOCIAL welfare initiatives, it is our number one GOAL to improve our COMMUNITIES and with your help EVERYONE has the chance to SHINE.

★ macy's
GIVES

heart of the community

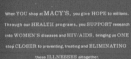

When YOU shop at MACY'S, you give HOPE to millions. Through our HEALTH programs, you SUPPORT research into WOMEN'S diseases and HIV/AIDS, bringing us ONE step CLOSER to preventing, treating and ELIMINATING these ILLNESSES altogether.

★ macy's
GIVES

a stroke of genius

Every time YOU shop at MACY'S, you bring the WORLD home. Through our ARTS programs, you GIVE our COMMUNITY the chance to EXPERIENCE creative works of all mediums and INSPIRE people to CREATE masterpieces of their own.

★ macy's
GIVES

the hero of the story

When YOU shop at MACY'S, you help CHILDREN in the COMMUNITY. Through our EDUCATION and LITERACY programs, you give them the CHANCE to learn WONDERFUL new things and the OPPORTUNITY to SUCCEED in all their LIFE'S ambitions.

★ macy's
GIVES

123

MACY'S GIVES • Macy's Gives is Macy's corporate giving program. These posters and advertisements were designed to highlight the many aspects of the company's corporate giving philosophy, all deeply rooted in diversity and inclusiveness with a particular focus on supporting the arts and cultural organizations. Macy's famous star logo served as the decorative and mnemonic element. **DESIGN FIRM:** Wink **ART DIRECTOR:** Scott Thares, Richard Boynton **DESIGNER AND ILLUSTRATOR:** Scott Thares **PHOTOGRAPHER:** Stock **CLIENT:** Macy's **PRIMARY FONT:** Steinweiss Script

DECORATIVE

FEELS LIKE PINS AND NEEDLES IN MY HEART • The contrast between the heavy letterforms and their "razor-sharp" counters was inspired by the shapes of old razor blades. The glyphs were digitally rendered and then printed in order to be hand-distressed.
DESIGNER AND ILLUSTRATOR: Bonnie Clas
PRIMARY FONT: Custom lettering

IRON GIANTS • The typography suggests the influence of Constructivism and late Futurism. The imagery, however, is postmodern in its overtly chaotic aspect.
DESIGN FIRM: *Wired* magazine
CREATIVE DIRECTOR: Scott Dadich **DESIGN DIRECTOR:** Wyatt Mitchell **DESIGNERS:** Scott Dadich, Carl Detorres **ILLUSTRATOR:** The Designers Republic **PHOTOGRAPHER:** Thomas Hannich **PUBLISHER:** Condé Nast **PRIMARY FONT:** Custom

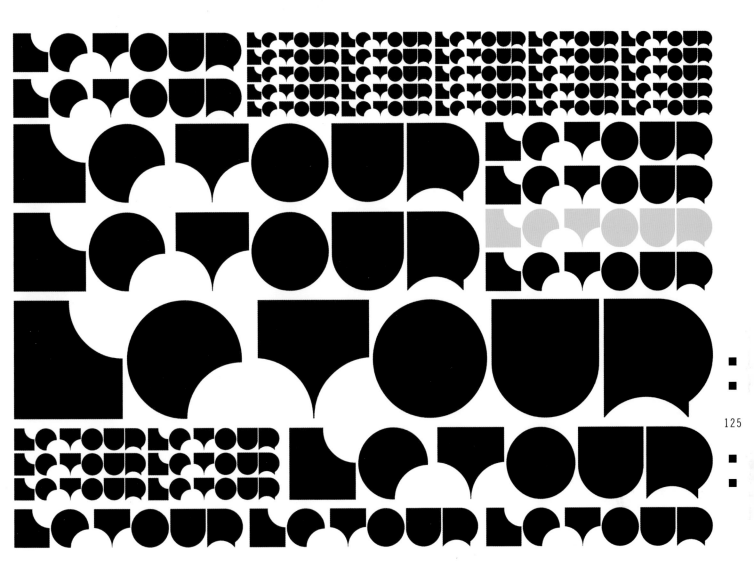

125

LE TOUR • These decorative letterforms depict the shapes of the wheels of multiple bicycles racing tightly together. Project "Le Tour" looks at the world's greatest bicycle race, the Tour de France, through the lense of photographer Brent Humphreys. The typeface and the logo were created to brand the project, gallery shows, and related products. **DESIGN FIRM:** TBA+D **DESIGNER:** Tom Brown (TBA+D) **CLIENT:** Brent Humphreys Photography **PRIMARY FONT:** Le Tour Display

DECORATIVE

JERRY LEE LEWIS • The opening spread for this magazine article on pioneer rocker Jerry Lee Lewis was influenced by vintage rockabilly concert posters, to which the designer added a contemporary decorative flair. **DESIGN DIRECTOR:** Fred Woodward **DESIGNER:** Drue Wagner **CLIENT:** *GQ* **PUBLISHER:** Condé Nast **PRIMARY FONT:** Sentinel

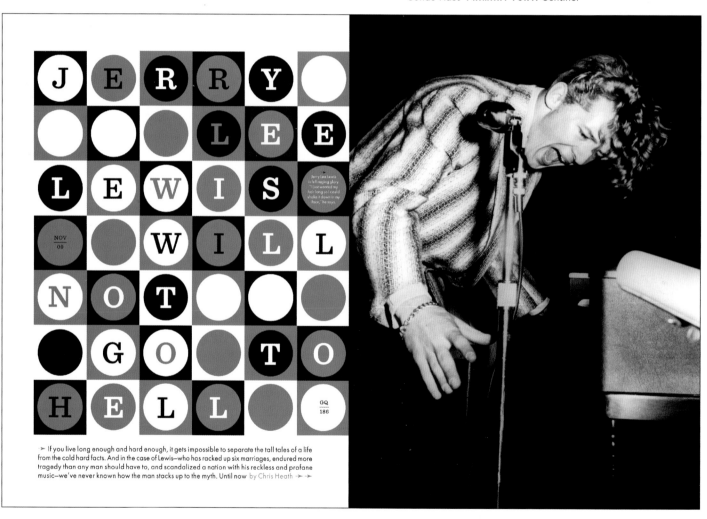

JERRY LEE LEWIS WILL NOT GO TO HELL

➤ If you live long enough and hard enough, it gets impossible to separate the tall tales of a life from the cold hard facts. And in the case of Lewis—who has racked up six marriages, endured more tragedy than any man should have to, and scandalized a nation with his reckless and profane music—we've never known how the man stacks up to the myth. Until now by Chris Heath ➤ ➤

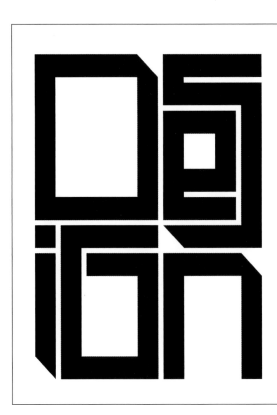

Design
ENTIRE ISSUE COVER SECTION SERVICE NON-CELEBRITY PROFILE
CELEBRITY/ENTERTAINMENT PROFILE NEWS/REPORTAGE
TRAVEL/FOOD STILL LIFE, FASHION/BEAUTY TRADE/CORPORATE
EDUCATIONAL/INSTITUTIONAL REDESIGN

SPD PUB 45 • In this book design for *SPD PUB 45*, the Society of Publication Designers' 45th annual, the serpentine lettering is easy to decipher. It conforms to the rectangular grid of the page and is a maze that requires untangling. **DESIGN FIRM:** TBA+D **DESIGNER:** Tom Brown (TBA+D) **CLIENT:** Society of Publication Designers **PRIMARY FONT:** Custom

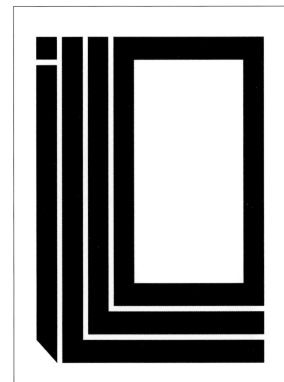

Illustration
COVER SPREAD OR SINGLE PAGE
ENTIRE STORY

DECORATIVE

RICHARD TYPE SPECIMEN •
Dirk Laucke notes that these type
specimen posters designed for Zeeburg
Type Foundry using the Richard
typeface, which Laucke created, are
not based on one person or design.
There is, however, a deliberate
historical resemblance to 19th-
century handmade samplers, used
as inspiration. **DESIGN FIRM:** Studio
Laucke Siebein **ART DIRECTORS:** Dirk
Laucke, Johanna Siebein **DESIGNERS:**
Dirk Laucke (type design), Johanna
Siebein **CLIENT:** Zeeburg Type
Foundry **PRIMARY FONTS:** Richard by
Dirk Laucke, Futura

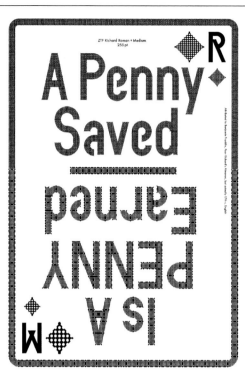

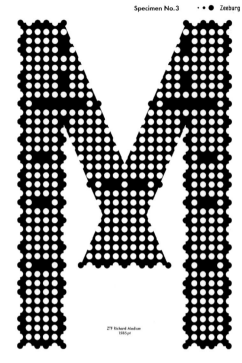

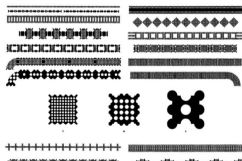

DECORATIVE

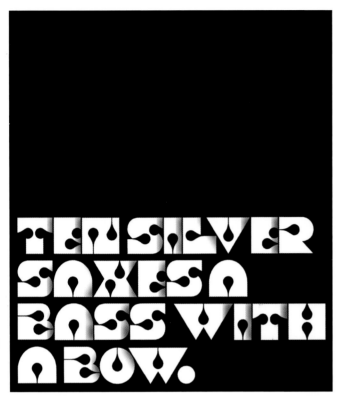

CINNAMON GIRL • This project came out of the designer's desire to illustrate some of her favorite lyrics from a song by Neil Young. "I designed the lettering as solid white forms before working out the bowls and counters," Bonnie Clas explains. "The ink-drop shapes gave the effect of fluidity that I was looking for to contrast with the chunky geometric letterforms." **DESIGNER AND ILLUSTRATOR:** Bonnie Clas **PRIMARY FONT:** Custom lettering

A.D.C. ISSUE 1 • Terry Koppel's design for the first issue of the Art Directors Club's quarterly journal was inspired by his own father's design work. It combines all the modern and eclectic traits of the late 1930s. **DESIGN FIRM:** T. Koppel Design **ART DIRECTOR AND DESIGNER:** Terry Koppel **PHOTOGRAPHER:** Photographs supplied **CLIENT:** Art Directors Club **PRIMARY FONTS:** Futura Bold, Miss Brooks

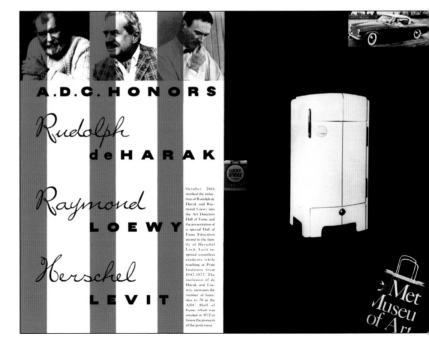

00:00

HOME		VISITOR
21		**02**

PERIOD
● ● ● ●

SIX PALE, EARTHBOUND DESK JOCKEYS FROM *GQ* CHALLENGED THE GREATEST BASKETBALL PLAYER ON EARTH, ALSO KNOWN AS **LeBRON JAMES**, TO A GAME OF BASKETBALL AT THE TIME AND PLACE OF HIS CHOOSING.

UNFORTUNATELY, THE CHALLENGE WAS ACCEPTED

BY
JOEL LOVELL

PHOTOGRAPHS BY
NATHANIEL GOLDBERG

LEBRON JAMES • The design of this magazine article on basketball player Lebron James is decorative in so far as its concept is inspired by vernacular signage. It is a classic basketball scoreboard, "derived from Fred Woodward's memory of his high school scoreboard," says Thomas Alaberty. **DESIGN DIRECTOR:** Fred Woodward **DESIGNER:** Thomas Alberty **PHOTOGRAPHER:** Nathaniel Goldberg **CLIENT:** *GQ* **PUBLISHER:** Condé Nast **PRIMARY FONT:** Titling Gothic

131

DECORATIVE

WE SING AS ONE • This image, designed for the cover of a record created by members of Trinity Grace Church in New York City, was influenced by old woodtype show posters. "A very diverse group of people come together for one purpose: to make a record," notes illustrator Jeff Rogers, "so I used the letters in the title to express that idea." **DESIGNER AND ILLUSTRATOR:** Jeff Rogers **CLIENT AND PUBLISHER:** Trinity Grace Church **PRIMARY FONTS:** Various

THE BOY FROM GITMO • In the opening spread of this article on mail censorship in military prisons, the typography becomes an illustration of censorship, both realistically and ornamentally. **DESIGN DIRECTOR:** Fred Woodward **DESIGNER:** Chelsea Cardinal **PHOTOGRAPHER:** Benjamin Lowry **CLIENT:** *GQ* **PUBLISHER:** Condé Nast **PRIMARY FONT:** Replica

KANT AND PHENOMENOLOGY • The jacket of this philosophy book, which contends that Kant's Constructivist approach to knowledge made him the first great phenomenologist, was inspired by the content of the book, rather than by a historical reference. "I wanted the word 'Kant' to be visibly constructed, caught in the act of appearing or coalescing into a word," says designer Isaac Tobin. **DESIGN FIRM:** The University of Chicago Press **ART DIRECTOR:** Jill Shimabukuro **DESIGNER:** Isaac Tobin **PUBLISHER:** The University of Chicago Press **PRIMARY FONTS:** Custom lettering, Belizio, Fournier

133

DECORATIVE

RIHANNA • The influences behind this magazine design are a combination of Futurist and Dada sensibilities. The complex simplicity of the letterforms suggests a hybrid approach to modernist tendencies. **DESIGN FIRM:** W magazine **ART DIRECTOR AND DESIGNER:** Nathalie Kirsheh **PHOTOGRAPHER:** Craig McDean **PUBLISHER:** Condé Nast **PRIMARY FONT:** Paz

134

SONY GLOBAL MAGAZINE • Terry Koppel calls this work "a modern interpretation of Russian Constructivism." **DESIGN FIRM:** T. Koppel Design **ART DIRECTOR AND DESIGNER:** Terry Koppel **PHOTOGRAPHER:** Ruven Afanador **CLIENT:** Sony **PRIMARY FONTS:** Alternate Gothic No. 2, Helvetica Cy, Helvetica Inserat Roman

PASSION • Commissioned to design a logotype for use on a calendar for which the theme was "passion," designer Paul Sych made letterforms that are ornamented with hearts. **DESIGN FIRM:** Faith **ART DIRECTOR AND DESIGNER:** Paul Sych **CLIENT:** Huge Paper Company **PRIMARY FONT:** Custom

JAMES BROWN • This genealogy-inspired opening spread for magazine *GQ* uses the ornamental qualities of a family tree. **DESIGN DIRECTOR:** Fred Woodward **DESIGNER:** Thomas Alberty **CLIENT:** *GQ* **PUBLISHER:** Condé Nast **PRIMARY FONTS:** Miller Display Italic, Titling Gothic

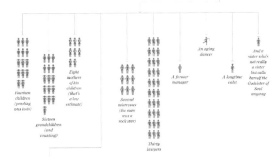

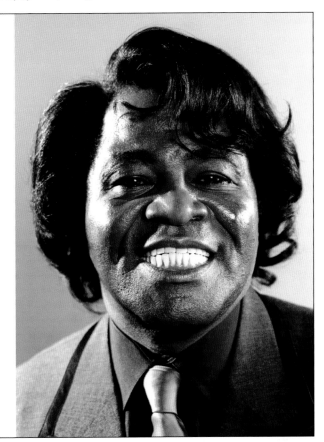

When James Brown died on Christmas Day 2006, he left behind a fortune worth tens, maybe hundreds, of millions of dollars. The problem is, he also left behind

All of whom want a piece of his legacy. And when the dust clears, there might be nothing left of the (supremely talented, extremely careless, and massively troubled) Godfather of Soul

Papa

by Sean Flynn

KINETIC

Modernist typography was viewed as a machine-age manifestation. Sans-serif types, although not born in the 20th century, were seen as a symbol of technology. Movement and the illusion of movement have been significant goals for many designers since machines made it possible to simulate and create movement on film, video, and now computer screens.

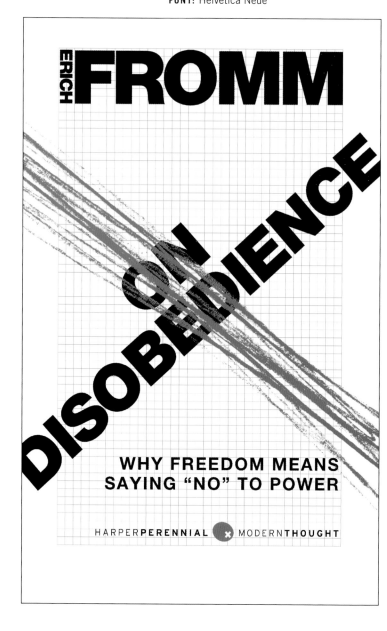

JOHNS HOPKINS FILM FESTIVAL • The sources of inspiration behind the design of this 2003 Johns Hopkins Film Festival poster combine Swiss styling and early 1960s eclecticism. **DESIGN FIRM:** Post Typography **ART DIRECTORS, DESIGNERS, AND ILLUSTRATORS:** Nolen Strals, Bruce Willen **CLIENT:** Johns Hopkins Film Festival **PRIMARY FONT:** Franklin Gothic

ON DISOBEDIENCE • For this philosophy series aimed at what Adam Johnson calls "hip smart readers," the designer was influenced by classic Swiss International Style posters. **DESIGN FIRM:** HarperCollins Publishers **ART DIRECTOR:** Milan Bozic **DESIGNER:** Adam Johnson **CLIENT:** Harper Perennial **PRIMARY FONT:** Helvetica Neue

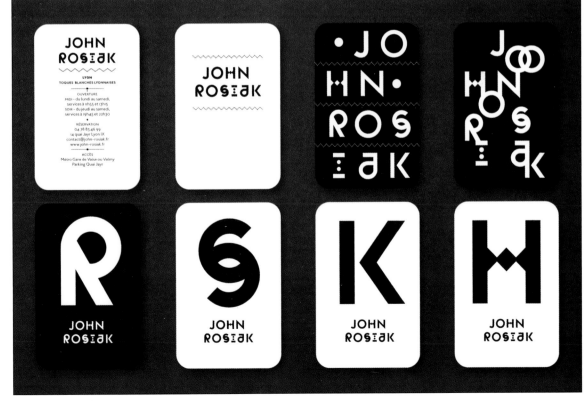

JOHN ROSIAK • John Rosiak is a French chef who is an adept of fusion cooking, mixing traditional French cuisine and molecular cooking. For this branding work, the designers wanted to create an identity that would translate both Rosiak's strong personality and his capacity for mad food combinations: (marshmallow and wine for dessert, for example). They were "inspired by the work of Schwitters and Dada to develop a kinetic font that immediately shows his creativity."
DESIGN FIRM: Müesli
ART DIRECTORS AND DESIGNERS: Léa Chapon, Mytil Ducomet **CLIENT:** Restaurant John Rosiak
PRIMARY FONTS: Font specially created by Müesli, ITC Johnston

KINETIC

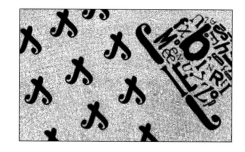

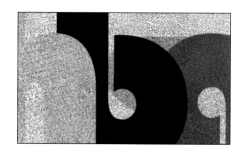

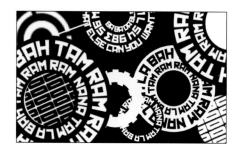

ELO TYPE VIDEO • "We were asked to create a type video using only typography based on a chosen song," says Kuczek. "I decided to create a type video commentary, using purely influences from the past. My inspiration came from various key posters in the history of graphic design, such as Russian Constructivism, Dada, and Bauhaus."
DESIGNER AND ILLUSTRATOR: Joanna Kuczek
CLIENT: MFA Design, School of Visual Arts
PRIMARY FONT: Found scanned type

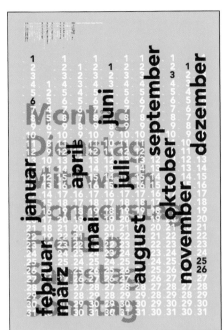

POSTER CALENDAR 2009 • "The poster is based on the typeface Avenir," explains Tim Sluiters. "The position of the month shows you what the first day of the month is. For example, in 2009, the first day of January was a Thursday, the first day of April was a Wednesday, and so on. The poster was designed in three different colors and influenced by a 1969 calendar by Prof. Hans (Nick) Roericht." **DESIGN FIRM:** timsluiters visuelle kommunikation **ART DIRECTOR AND DESIGNER:** Tim Sluiters **CLIENT:** Self **PRIMARY FONT:** Avenir by Adrian Frutiger (1988)

UNODC TRAINING POSTER • This is a series of typographic maps to help train the Russian police. The typographic solution was to build a simple world map from internationally recognized country abbreviation codes (GBR, USA, RU, etc.). **DESIGN FIRM:** Pentagram Design/London **DESIGNERS:** Harry Pearce, Jason Ching **PHOTOGRAPHER:** Nick Turner **CLIENT:** United Nations Office on Drugs and Crime **PRIMARY FONT:** Akzidenz-Grotesk

KINETIC

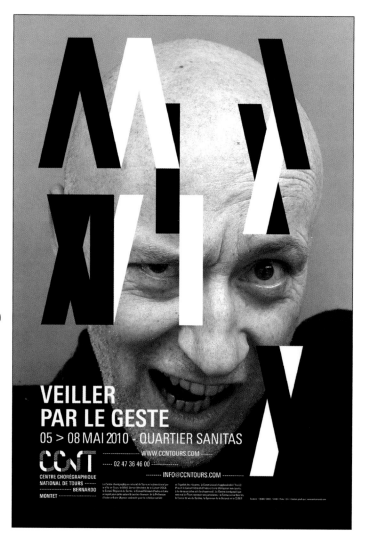

MENTORING PROGRAMM • The poster was designed for a program organized by HAWK (a German university) that helps women to successfully manage both their career and their family at the same time. It is printed (silkscreen) on real newspaper paper taken from the employment ads section of *Die Zeit*, the primary source for academic job adverts in Germany. **DESIGN FIRM:** Scrollan **ART DIRECTORS:** Anne-Lene Proff, Barbara Kotte, Peter Bünnagel **DESIGNER:** Anne-Lene Proff **CLIENT:** Hochschule für angewandte Wissenschaft und Kunst, Hildesheim **PRIMARY FONTS:** CG Alpin Gothic No. 3

VEILLER PAR LE GESTE • Commissioned to design a poster for a French National Choreographic Center, Müesli decided to create a kind of choreographic alphabet that, they say, "allowed us to make an invitation for everyone (not only dancers)." Abstracted forms of dance movements were turned into type and superimposed on the face of each dancer. A series of ten original combinations of type and face was generated to create different posters, flyers and invitations. **DESIGN FIRM:** Müesli **ART DIRECTORS AND DESIGNERS:** Léa Chapon, Mytil Ducomet **CLIENT:** Centre Chorégraphique National de Tours **PRIMARY FONT:** Linotype Univers

DELTA SPIRIT • This poster advertises Delta Spirit's 2010 concert in Columbus, Ohio. Working from the title of the band's debut album, *Ode to Sunshine*, Base Art Co. chose a literal interpretation, creating a shining sun with beams made out of the album's song lyrics. **DESIGN FIRM:** Base Art Co. **ART DIRECTOR:** Terry Rohrbach **DESIGNERS:** Terry Rohrbach, Drue Dixon **CLIENT:** PromoWest Productions **PRIMARY FONTS:** Trade Gothic, Knockout, Chronicle

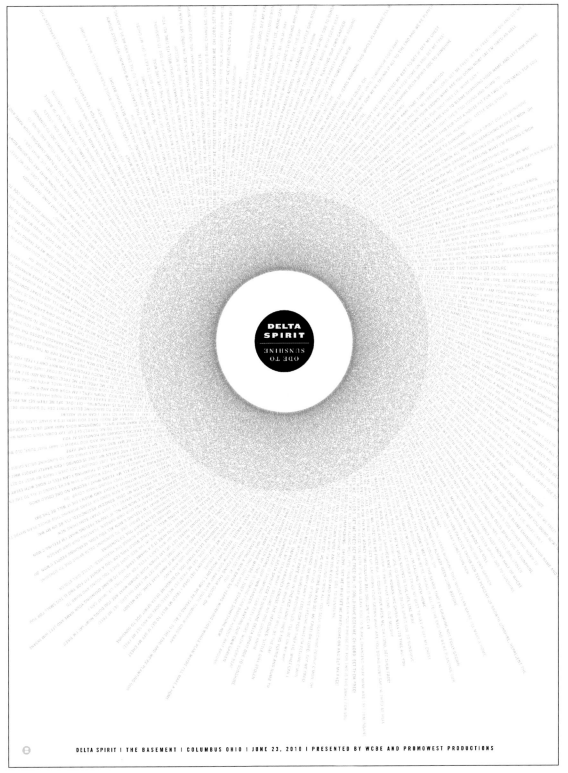

KINETIC

AFAA • Type and image move in a kind of syncopated ballet to give a sense of stasis and movement in this book cover design. **DESIGN FIRM:** Bureau 205 **ART DIRECTOR:** Damien Gautier **DESIGNERS:** Damien Gautier, Quentin Margat **PHOTOGRAPHER:** Didier Boy de la Tour **CLIENT:** AFAA **PRIMARY FONT:** Replica

BlueBolt:

Where design professionals and suppliers come together to **select, specify and organize**

More than 25 types of interior finishes. Over 40 (and counting) leading commercial brands. Search, select, specify, organize, save, share, and order samples from all of them. From your computer desktop.

What is it, anyway?

BlueBolt Studio is an easy-to-use software tool that simplifies and streamlines the specification process. Always available on your computer desktop, BlueBolt Studio lets you work with color-true product images and accurate specifications for more than 25 types of interior finishes and over 40 (and counting) leading commercial brands.

TRY IT FREE:
WWW.BLUEBOLT.COM
CALL BLUEBOLT:
(866) 865-2600

BLUEBOLT • BlueBolt Studio is an identity and communication program that includes a software suite and online tools conceived for the architectural and interior design markets. For this project, Alexander Isley, Inc. created the logo and consulted on product naming. They also developed web-based interfaces, exhibits, printed materials, and promotion. The aesthetic was influenced by old Herman Miller ads, El Lissitzky, Lester Beall, and Herbert Matter. **DESIGN FIRM:** Alexander Isley, Inc. **ART DIRECTOR:** Alexander Isley **DESIGNER:** Liesl Kaplan **CLIENT:** BlueBolt Networks, Durham **PRIMARY FONT:** Trade Gothic

CODEX • This exhibition catalog was designed to promote an exhibition of interesting editorial projects curated by Manystuff & Hypertexte in Toulouse, France. The type here has a static quality, while the orientation of the page layout forces the viewer to move. **DESIGN FIRM:** Pierre Vanni **ART DIRECTOR AND DESIGNER:** Pierre Vanni **CLIENT:** Manystuff & Hypertexte **PRIMARY FONTS:** Typ1451 (lineto), OCR-A

KINETIC

RE-DESIGNING THE EAST • "Cutting" the type to suggest a collage of violently severed messages evokes movement and disruption. **DESIGN FIRM:** L2M3 Kommunikationsdesign GmbH **ART DIRECTOR:** Sascha Lobe **DESIGNERS:** Sascha Lobe, Dirk Wachowiak **CLIENT:** Württembergischer Kunstverein Stuttgart **PRIMARY FONTS:** Monotype Grotesque, Helvetica Neue

144

MASSIN • Although Eugène Ionesco's *The Bald Soprano* (or *La Cantatrice Chauve*) is the most well-known design by Massin outside of France, only a few commonly reproduced spreads appear in design history books. "We decided to print the complete book on the front of the poster," says Mirko Ilić. "And if you follow the directions on the back of the poster, you can cut and assemble it into a mini replica of the book. The Cooper Union's exhibition space was set up almost like a spiral or a labyrinth, so we used that idea to set up a visual spiral on the poster that ends with Massin's name. The idea was that the viewer walks through the exhibition and in the end finds out about Massin..." **DESIGN FIRM:** Mirko Ilić Corp. **ART DIRECTOR:** Mirko Ilić **DESIGNERS:** Mirko Ilić, Heath Hinegardner **CLIENT:** The Cooper Union, Future Flair **PRIMARY FONT:** Champion

KINETIC

GEORGES ADILON: ARTISTE & ARCHITECTE • The type for this exhibition poster about George Adilon's work as artist and architect is static, but the positioning of the words on the picture speeds up the eye-tracking movement. **DESIGN FIRM:** Bureau 205 **ART DIRECTOR:** Damien Gautier **DESIGNER:** Damien Gautier, Quentin Margat **PHOTOGRAPHER:** Blaise Adilon **CLIENT:** Musée d'Art Contemporain de Lyon, BF15, CAUE, Lycée Sainte-Marie **PRIMARY FONT:** Knockout

PARC ARCHITECTES • To let clients of Parc Architectes know that this young architecture studio was about to finish its first big project, Müesli decided to create a large greeting card, which eventually became a poster. Müesli focused on a "simple design that could clearly refer to the building (an auditorium) and would be easy to silkscreen. We created all the design with the four faces of the building, producing a modular approach that reflects its spirit." They were influenced by Oscar Niemeyer's Brasilia architecture, the Bauhaus, and Josef Müller-Brockmann. **DESIGN FIRM:** Müesli **ART DIRECTORS AND DESIGNERS:** Léa Chapon, Mytil Ducomet **CLIENT:** Parc Architectes, Paris **PRIMARY FONT:** Linotype Univers

THE CHEESE STANDS ALONE • This poster for a lecture hosted by the New Mexico Advertising Federation has its messages flying all over, and yet contained within the main letterforms. **DESIGN FIRM:** Alexander Isley, Inc. **ART DIRECTOR AND DESIGNER:** Alexander Isley **PRIMARY FONTS:** Filosofia, Akzidenz-Grotesk

KINETIC

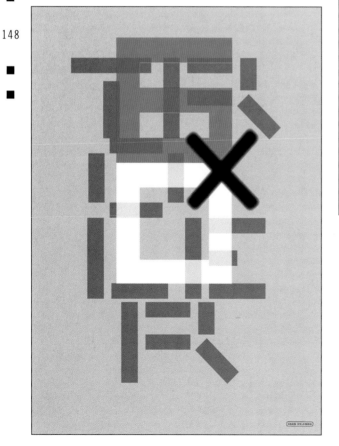

TROXLER: 60 • Several designers were invited to create a poster page to celebrate the 60th birthday of designer Niklaus Troxler. Carin Goldberg submitted several kinetic options, in which type, geometric bands, and splotches are used to suggest an ad hoc sensibility. **DESIGN FIRM:** Carin Goldberg Design **ART DIRECTOR AND DESIGNER:** Carin Goldberg **CLIENT:** Friends of Niklaus Troxler **PRIMARY FONT:** Manual typewriter

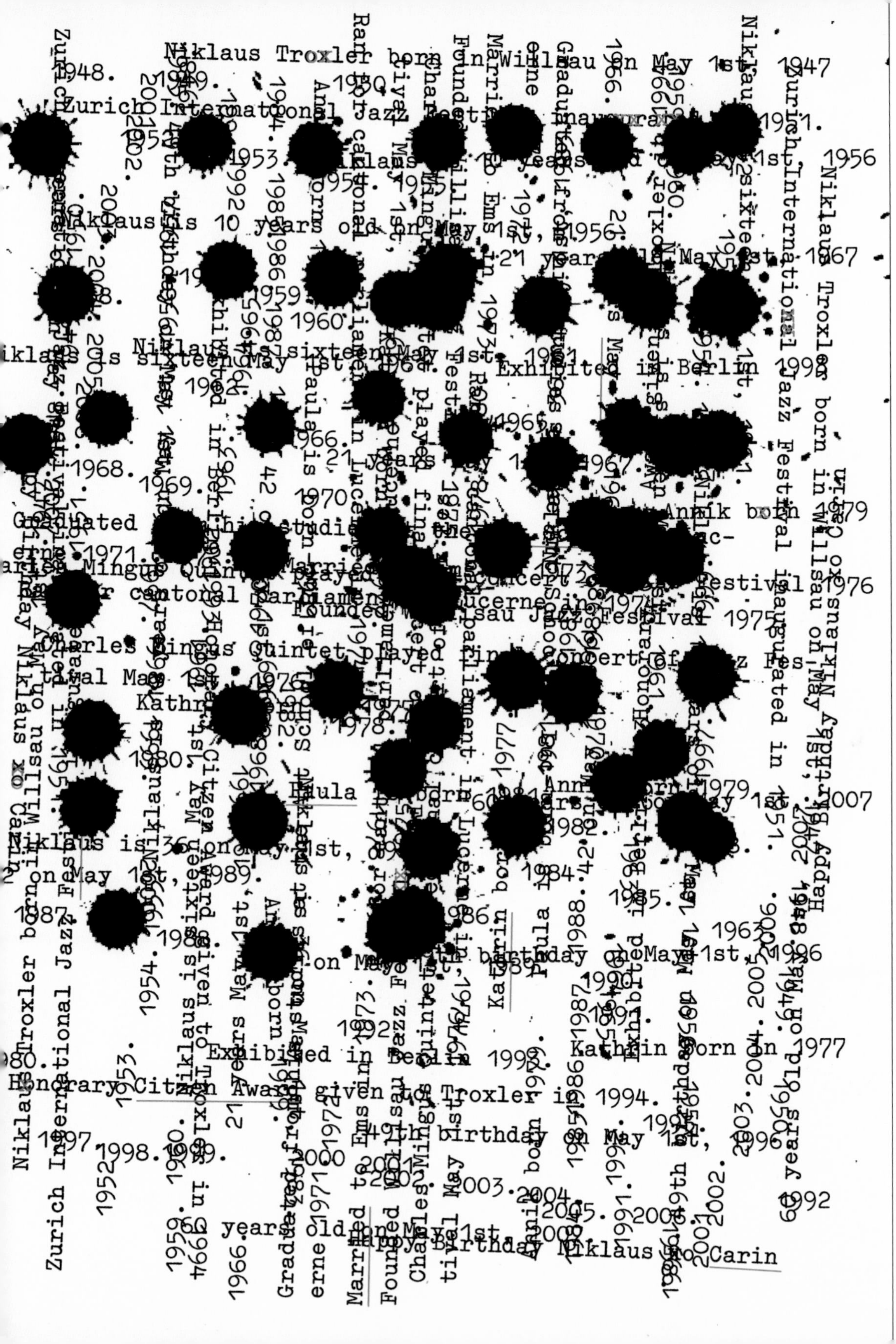

Niklaus Troxler born on May 1st, 1947

Zurich International Jazz Festival inaugurated in 1951.

Niklaus is 10 years old on May 1st, 1956.

Exhibited in Berlin

Niklaus is sixteen May 1st,

Graduated

Charles Mingus Quintet played first concert of Jazz Fes-

Founded Willisau Jazz Festival 1975

Annik born 1976

1968. 1969. 1970. 1971.

Niklaus Troxler born in Willisau on May 1st, 1947.

Happy Birthday Niklaus & Carin

Kathrin born on 1977

Happy Birthday Niklaus & Carin

149

KINETIC

KANYE WEST • The orientation of the vertical headline – one line down and the other up – accentuates the kinetic quality of the image in this composition for magazine *GQ*. **DESIGN DIRECTOR:** Fred Woodward **DESIGNER:** Anton Loukhnovets **PHOTOGRAPHER:** Nathaniel Goldberg **CLIENT:** *GQ* **PUBLISHER:** Condé Nast **PRIMARY FONT:** Akkurat Mono

150

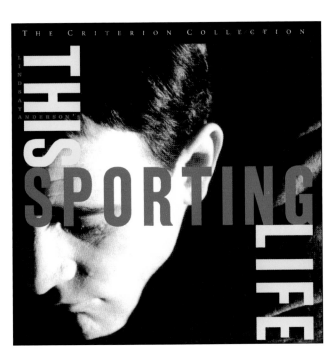

THIS SPORTING LIFE • The stairstep typographic orientation of this headline, influenced by the Bauhaus and Russian Constructivist styles, adds motion to the solemnly static image. **DESIGN FIRM:** T. Koppel Design **ART DIRECTOR AND DESIGNER:** Terry Koppel **PHOTOGRAPHER:** Theatrical Publicity Photos/Movie Stills **CLIENT:** The Criterion Collection **PRIMARY FONT:** Koppel's Woodblock Condensed

RAY OZZIE HAS A PLAN • The Russian Constructivist influence can be seen quite clearly in this example of diagonal design. The angle of the type and borders implies motion, while the vertical central line adds visual tension. **DESIGN FIRM:** *Wired* magazine **CREATIVE DIRECTOR AND DESIGNER:** Scott Dadich **PHOTOGRAPHER:** Lionel Deluy **PUBLISHER:** Condé Nast **PRIMARY FONT:** Tungsten

KINETIC

MYSTERIUM FIDEI • "Mysterium fidei" translates as "the mystery of faith" and Bonnie Clas created the lettering to reflect overlapping religious symbols stripped to their most basic graphic forms. The "M" in particular was inspired by the structure of a church (frontal view). It also became the main illustration for the type-specimen poster, which is based on religious iconography and ecclesiastical architecture. **DESIGNER AND ILLUSTRATOR:** Bonnie Clas **PRIMARY FONT:** Custom lettering

HOFER WANTED • Slicing type to obscure some of the letters (but without rendering them illegible) is not always a sign of movement but it does imply a quick cutting hand. **DESIGN FIRM:** L2M3 Kommunikationsdesign GmbH **ART DIRECTOR:** Sascha Lobe **DESIGNERS:** Sascha Lobe, Dirk Wachowiak, Sven Thiery **PHOTOGRAPHER:** Brigida González **CLIENT:** Tiroler Landesmuseum Ferdinandeum, Innsbruck **PRIMARY FONTS:** Conduit ITC, Univers

LUMPEN MAGAZINE • The influences here are a kinetic melange of modernism, Russian Constructivism, punk-rock aesthetic, Wolfgang Weingart, DYI, Alexey Brodovitch, Non-Format, Ludovic Balland, fashion editorials, and copy machines – or what might be called "mix-master modern." **DESIGN FIRM:** Plural **ART DIRECTORS AND DESIGNERS:** Jeremiah Chiu, Renata Graw **ILLUSTRATORS:** Andy Buckholder, Jeremiah Chiu, Renata Graw **PHOTOGRAPHERS:** Anticon, Aron Gent, Renata Graw **CLIENT:** Public Media Institute **PRIMARY FONTS:** Custom type, Golden Type, Univers, Bodoni, NE10

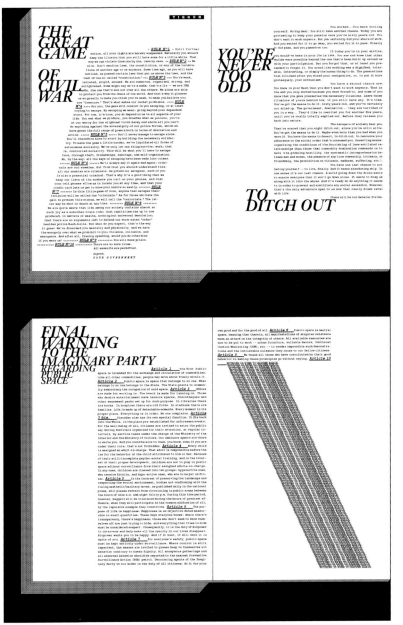

KINETIC

LUMPEN MAGAZINE • Another example of "mix-master modern" frenetically absorbing many design influences at once. **DESIGN FIRM:** Plural **ART DIRECTORS AND DESIGNERS:** Jeremiah Chiu, Renata Graw **ILLUSTRATORS:** Andy Buckholder, Jeremiah Chiu, Renata Graw **PHOTOGRAPHERS:** Anticon, Aron Gent, Renata Graw **CLIENT:** Public Media Institute **PRIMARY FONTS:** Custom type, Golden Type, Univers, Bodoni, NE10

DESIGN AUS DDORF • The custom-developed dot-type system is based on the typeface Avenir by Adrian Frutiger. "The special thing about the poster is that you can read it better from a distance than when you are near," notes Tim Sluiters. "The idea was to create a poster that would look very exciting from a close distance but just informative from afar." **DESIGN FIRM:** timsluiters visuelle kommunikation **ART DIRECTOR:** Tim Sluiters **DESIGNER:** Tim Sluiters **CLIENT:** University of Applied Sciences, Düsseldorf **PRIMARY FONT:** Custom

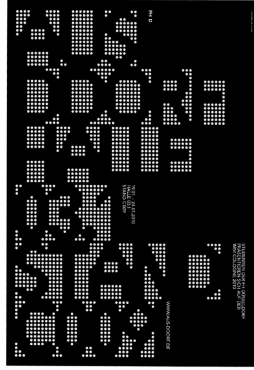

AFTERTASTE 2 ·

Aftertaste is a series of lectures and roundtable conversations dedicated to the critical review of interior design and the identification of contemporary issues that will challenge practitioners in the near future. The off-register color evokes offset-printing technology, Knoll posters, and kaleidoscopes. **DESIGN FIRM:** Instance **ART DIRECTOR:** Meg Callery **DESIGNER:** Lisa Maione **CLIENT:** Parsons **PRIMARY FONT:** Akkurat

AFT ERT AST E 2

Jay Bernstein
James Casebere
Kent Kleinman
Emmanuelle Linard
Julie Lasky
Joanna Merwood-Salisbury
Stephen and Timothy Quay
Courtney Smith
Penny Sparke
Ioanna Theocharopoulou
Anthony Vidler
Lois Weinthal
Allan Wexler
Mark Wigley
Alfred Zolligner

AFTERTASTE 2
New Agendas for the Study of the Interior
April 4 & 5, 2008
Department of Architecture, Interior Design, and Lighting
PARSONS THE NEW SCHOOL FOR DESIGN

Anna-Maria Stephen Kellen Auditorium
Sheila C. Johnson Design Center
66 Fifth Avenue New York City

Aftertaste 2 is made possible by the generous support of ***

Friday, April 4	Saturday, April 5	
2:00–6:00 p.m.	10:00 a.m.–2:00 p.m.	3:00–7:00 p.m.
The Intellectual History of Taste	*Representing the Interior*	*The Narrative Life of Things*

KINETIC

DREIDIMENSIONALE KOMMUNIKATION • This poster was created to announce the guest lectures of the candidates for the three-dimensional communication professorship. The first four letters of "Kommunikation," divided from the rest of the word, have another meaning: KOMM means COME. The main intention was to animate the students to "KOMM" (come) to the lectures. The poster was designed in three different colors. **DESIGN FIRM:** timsluiters visuelle kommunikation **ART DIRECTOR AND DESIGNER:** Tim Sluiters **CLIENT:** University of Applied Sciences, Düsseldorf **PRIMARY FONT:** Helvetica

156

IDEA MAGAZINE • Design firm Tomato wrote and designed this moving 144-page essay on the creative processes behind their work with Underworld for Japanese design magazine *Idea*. **DESIGN FIRM:** Tomato **ART DIRECTOR AND PHOTOGRAPHER:** John Warwicker **DESIGNERS:** John Warwicker, Yoshihisa Shira (Japanese typography) **CLIENT:** *Idea* magazine **PUBLISHER:** Seibundo Shinkosha **PRIMARY FONT:** Baskerville

KINETIC

 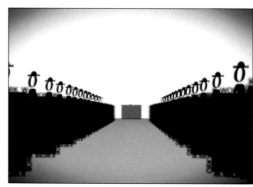

MODERN WORLD • Cristina Vasquez's animation depicts a world inspired by futurist movies such as *Metropolis* (1927). In this black and white music video, "I used repetition as an element for rhythm and built a world of type where uniformity, conflict, and the urban city become too much for some to handle," she explains. **DESIGN FIRM:** MFA Design, School of Visual Arts **ART DIRECTOR AND DESIGNER:** Cristina Vasquez **PRIMARY FONT:** P22 Modernist Pack

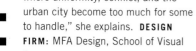

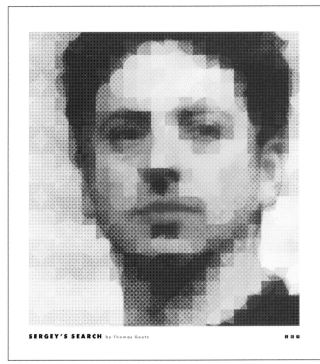

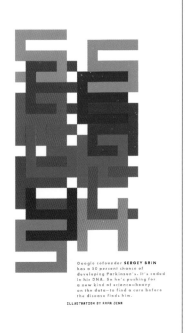

SERGEY'S SEARCH • Overlapping types in multiple colors and hues are bound to make the eye jump out of its socket and to trigger a sensation of movement. **DESIGN FIRM:** *Wired* magazine **CREATIVE DIRECTOR AND DESIGNER:** Scott Dadich **ILLUSTRATOR:** Rafa Jenn **PUBLISHER:** Condé Nast **PRIMARY FONT:** Luggage

SKYSCRAPER, I LOVE YOU • This book with Karl Hyde (of British electronic group Underworld) is a typographic journey and exploration inspired by Warwicker's and Hyde's walks through the streets of New York. **DESIGN FIRM:** Tomato **ART DIRECTOR AND DESIGNER:** John Warwicker **CLIENT:** Underworld **PUBLISHER:** Booth-Clibborn Editions **PRIMARY FONTS:** Various styles and weights of Compacta, Helvetica Inserat, Clarendon, Impact, and Bureau Grotesque – all modified by being processed via thermal fax and multiple overprinting.

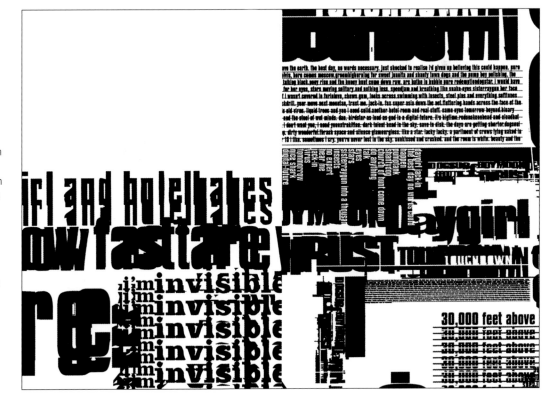

KINETIC

THE SAATCHI DECADE • Layering image and type in foreground and background colors with seemingly random combinations of weights is a hallmark of kineticism. **DESIGN FIRM:** Barnbrook **ART DIRECTOR AND DESIGNER:** Jonathan Barnbrook **CLIENT:** Saatchi Gallery **PUBLISHER:** Booth-Clibborn Editions **PRIMARY FONT:** Courier

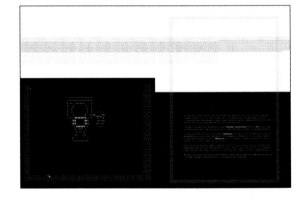

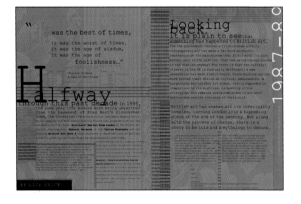

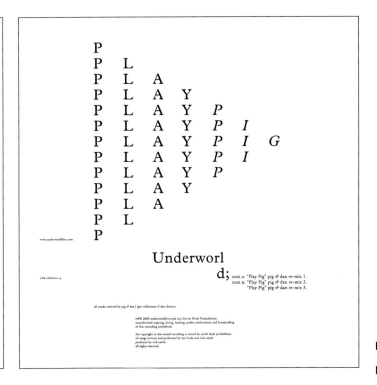

www.underworldlive.com

uwr010

Underworl
d; side a1: "Play Pig" *buick* project re-mix 1.   remix and additional production by nic fanciulli & andy chatterley.
side b1: "Play Pig" *buick* project re-mix 2.   remix and additional production by nic fanciulli & andy chatterley.
side b2: "Play Pig" Underworld *ritornan* version.

(P)© 2005 underworldlive.com (c/o Sastre Hyrst Productions).
unauthorised copying, hiring, lending, public performance and broadcasting
of this recording prohibited.
the copyright in this sound recording is owned by smith hyde productions.
all songs written and performed by karl hyde and rick smith.
produced by rick smith.
all rights reserved.

www.underworldlive.com

uwr-060002-4

Underworl
d; SIDE A: "Play Pig" *pig & dan re-mix* 1.
SIDE B: "Play Pig" *pig & dan re-mix* 2.
"Play Pig" *pig & dan re-mix* 3.

all tracks remixed by pig & dan | igor schkomoa & dan duncan.

(P)© 2005 underworldlive.com (c/o Sastre Hyrst Productions).
unauthorised copying, hiring, lending, public performance and broadcasting
of this recording prohibited.
the copyright in this sound recording is owned by smith hyde productions.
all songs written and performed by karl hyde and rick smith.
produced by rick smith.
all rights reserved.

PLAY PIG • The influences for this 12"-vinyl sleeve design are Apollinaire's *Calligrammes*, 1960s Concrete poetry, and Bob Cobbing. **DESIGN FIRM:** Tomato **ART DIRECTOR AND DESIGNER:** John Warwicker **CLIENT:** Underworld **PUBLISHER:** Junior Boy's Own **PRIMARY FONT:** Fournier

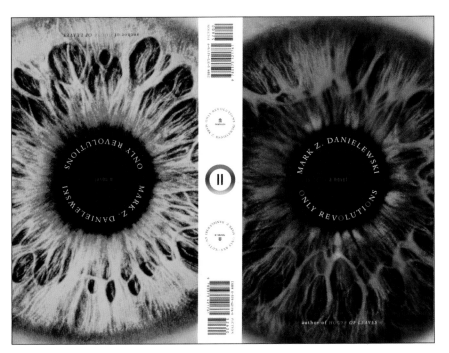

ONLY REVOLUTIONS • This book reads from both sides to the center, with 360 words per page, and the author insisted on using an eye as cover art. "The objective," says Archie Ferguson, "was to create an unusual package that has no front and no back." **DESIGN FIRM:** Archie Ferguson Design **ART DIRECTOR AND DESIGNER:** Archie Ferguson **PHOTOGRAPHER:** Ellen Martorelli/Getty Images **CLIENT:** Pantheon Books **PRIMARY FONT:** Dante

KINETIC

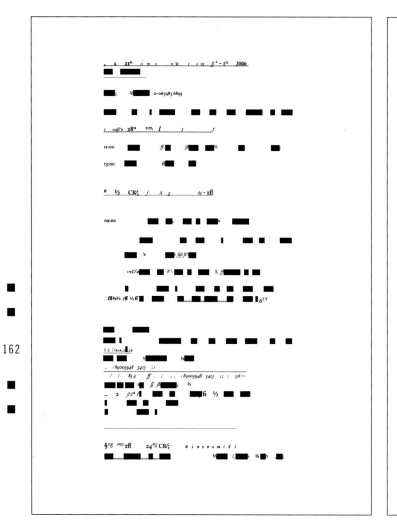

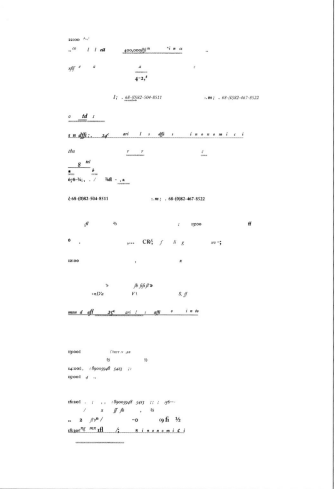

MISCOMMUNICATION 1 & 2 • "These designs from the exhibition 'August' were inspired by the rebuilt version of a corrupted email," says Simon Taylor. **DESIGN FIRM:** Tomato **DESIGNER:** Simon Taylor **CLIENT:** Reed Space Gallery, Tokyo **PRIMARY FONT:** Bodoni

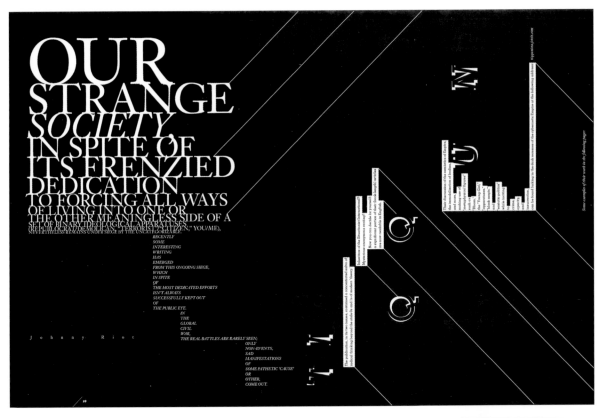

LUMPEN MAGAZINE • Using multiple sizes of smashed type is a common way of suggesting movement on a static page.
DESIGN FIRM: Plural **ART DIRECTORS AND DESIGNERS:** Jeremiah Chiu, Renata Graw **ILLUSTRATORS:** Andy Buckholder, Jeremiah Chiu, Renata Graw **PHOTOGRAPHERS:** Anticon, Aron Gent, Renata Graw **CLIENT:** Public Media Institute **PRIMARY FONTS:** Custom type, Golden Type, Univers, Bodoni, NE10

KINETIC

THE WHISTLER • Armin Hofmann, Ludovic Balland, Wolfgang Weingart, punk rock, and DIY aesthetics are among the influences for *The Whistler* – a broadsheet documenting the work behind Plural's storefront installation at The Whistler, a bar in Chicago. Sections include initial ideas, proposals, interviews, inventories, and statistical information. The verso of the publication plays with certain objects used at the bar, expressing some of the rhythm involved in bartending. **DESIGN FIRM:** Plural **ART DIRECTORS AND DESIGNERS:** Jeremiah Chiu, Renata Graw **ILLUSTRATOR:** Plural **PHOTOGRAPHER:** Shannon Benine **CLIENT:** The Whistler, Chicago **PRIMARY FONT:** Mercury

164

Di, Do–So: 11–18 Uhr, Mi: 11–20 Uhr
www.wkv-stuttgart.de

Württembergischer Kunstverein Stuttgart
Schlossplatz 2, D–70173 Stuttgart

KUNST UND GESELLSCHAFT

KUNST UND GESELLSCHAFT • The bars on this poster, undulating under the type, give a vivid impression of motion. **DESIGN FIRM:** L2M3 Kommunikationsdesign GmbH **ART DIRECTOR:** Sascha Lobe **DESIGNERS:** Ina Bauer, Marvin Boiko, Sascha Lobe **CLIENT:** Württembergischer Kunstverein Stuttgart **PRIMARY FONTS:** Monotype Grotesque, SuperGroteskA

Anja Abele · Claudia Bosch · Petra Breitenbücher · Gisela Aichholz · Petra Sybille App · Wolfgang Brenneisen · Barbara Armbruster · A-Team · Felix Burgel · Esky Bail · Sibylle Burr · Andreas Bär · Regine Bartholdt · Prof. Klaus Bushoff · David Baur · Bedriye Caliskan · Ingeborg Benz · Stefan Cante · Ulrike Berg · Nicole Daudert · Rudi Beutinger · Wolfgang M. Dehm · Dagmar Binanzer-Kraus · Anita Dieter · Friedemann Blum · Klaus Dietrich · Renate Bogatke · Elin Doka · Josephine Bonnet · Andrea Drechsel · Albrecht A. Bopp · Christa Duvell

Renata Earnshaw · Björn Gebhard · Martin-Ulrich Ehret · Martina Geiger-Gerlach · Edith Eidner · Carola Gera-Staber · Gert Eisner · Arlette Gerlach · Susanne Engelke · Beatrix Giebel · Hannelore Fehse · Margit Gillé · Susanne Feix · Christa Gipser · Barbara Fernandes · Gotthard Glitsch · Gerhard Walter Feuchter · Christine Glock-Ruhing · Dagmar Feuerstein · Hans A. Graef · Dorothea Fleiss · Doris Graf · Sara Focke-Levin · Renate Gross · Gudrun Freder · Kurt Grunow · Christoph Frick · Kristin Maria Hachenberg · Eva Friedrich · Ilse Hammerbacher · Andreas Futter · Hans-Rudolf Harder · Angela Garry · Erika Hart

Ingolf Jännsch · Rolf Hausberg · Ulrich Jerrentrup · Frank Hausmann · Almut Kaiser · Thomas Heger · Tamara Kappl · Arlette Heise · Gunther Kerbes · Wolf Helzle · Gerhard Killet · Michael Hermann · Peter Koch · Annette Hermann · Maria Kottwitz · Sigrid Anne Herold · Susanne Krüger-Eisenblätter · Helga Hess-Feldbach · Salla Kuhmo · Klaus Heuser · Christian Lang · Ulli Heyd · Raul Lopez Garcia · Angela Hildebrandt · Anja Luithle · Julia Hillesheim · Peter Magiera · Frank N. Hoffmann · Nana Hülsewig · Harald Huss · Wolfram Isele

Irene Müller · Christa Munkert · Dorothee Nestel · Wolfgang Neufang · Jeanette Oehlers · Anna Ottmann · Dieter Paul · Eva Paulitsch · Cerise Pelletier · Joachim Peter · Edith Raab · Christina Redenbacher-Merkelt · Beate Reflinghaus · Ilka Rehberger · Sieglinde Reiche · Susa Reinhardt · Heinz Renke

Gerold Reutter · Imelda Ruch · Frank Ulrich Rückert · Tobias Ruppert · Maria Grazia Sacchitelli · Michaela Sadlowski-Druzovic · Chieko Sasaki · Hiua Schasuar · Lucia Schautz · Gisela Schellenberger · Yvonne Schenk · Marko Schiefelbein · Hans K. Schlegel · Sigrun C. Schiebeck · Eva Schmeckenbecher · Anne-Katrin Schmid · Ulrich Schmidt

Volker Schöbel · Renate Schöck · Luise Scholl · Anne Schubert · Thorsten Schuberth · Ingrid Schütz · Jörg Michael Schulz · Behnam Shahbazy · Peter Schumann · Ulrich Seibt · Uwe H. Seyl · Elisabeth Smolarz · Diethard Sohn · Juliane Spitta · Rudi Sporer · Respektrum · Stef Stagel · Gudrun Staiger

Aurélie Staiger · Thomas Stanovic · Martina Staudenmayer · Renate Strauß · Christiane Thelen-Sthinee · Stefan Tümpel · Jutta Uhde · Thomas Ulm · Andrej Vaganov · Valentina Vaganov · Marinus van Aalst · Steffen Vetterle · VIOLA · Dorothee von Glinski · Vanja Vukovic · Veronika Weigel · Martina Weik

Hannelore Weitbrecht · Julia Wenz · Thilo Westermann · Oliver Wetterauer · Uta Weyrich · Stella Vera Wiedemann · Sylvia Winkler · Joachim Wörner · Ute Woracek · Xin-Yi Zhou · Annette Ziegler · Danielle Zimmermann · Andreas Zoller · Andrea Zug

Kunst und Gesellschaft
Ausstellung der Künstlermitglieder
20. Februar – 7. März 2010
Württembergischer Kunstverein Stuttgart

KINETIC

IN THE BELLY OF ST PAUL • Calligram-inspired typography for a book by John Warwicker and Karl Hyde (Underworld) that explores London through Karl's words. **DESIGN FIRM:** Tomato **ART DIRECTOR AND DESIGNER:** John Warwicker **CLIENT:** Underworld **PUBLISHER:** Underworld Print **PRIMARY FONTS:** Bureau Grotesque, Gill Sans, Bodoni, Clarendon, Caslon, Compacta, Impact

166

My love for you
My loſs of you

Reaching to touch

IS CONTANT

Through this night

THIS winter

i miss you

yet

you may never

discover this

I AM IN **AWE**

At the beauty of you

All

Receeding into dark ſtreets AGAIN

The cracks between
The brick around
The lights inside
Carrying you with me
Alone AGAIN
AGAIN

&

AGAIN

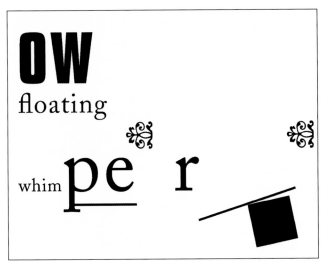

OW
floating
whim pe r

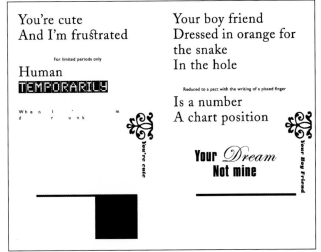

You're cute
And I'm frustrated

For limited periods only

Human
TEMPORARILY

When I ' m
d r u n k

You're cute

Your boy friend
Dressed in orange for
the snake
In the hole

Reduced to a pact with the writing of a pissed finger

Is a number
A chart position

Your *Dream*
Not mine

Your Boy Friend

EEZER

G

WITH HIS HEAD SHOWING THROUGH

Geezer with his head showin through

the top of his hair bending to his boots in a hiking jump and naked forearms Bicycle goalie boy in white and anorak with a garland of white flowers Tiny dangling things from his neck adjusts his gears stopping all stations Jammed between the sliding standing between the blue velveteen Looking crazy smiling at me with his bicycle red thing with dropped handlebars and tiny rucksack tidy sleeping bag thing.

London
September
1996

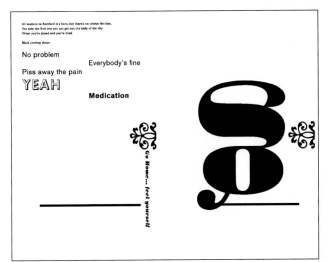

All stations to Romford is a bore, but there's no choice this fate.
You take the first one you can get out the belly of the city
When you're pissed and you're tired

Black cowboy shoes

No problem

Everybody's fine

Piss away the pain
YEAH

Medication

Go Home... feel yourself

§
ø

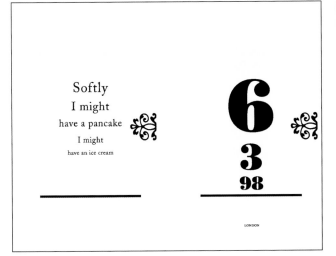

Softly

I might

have a pancake

I might

have an ice cream

6
3
98

LONDON

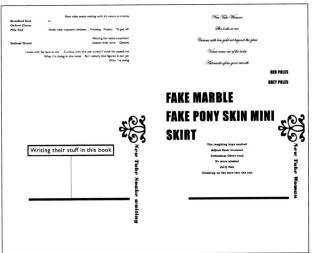

New tube snake waiting with it's doors in drizzle

Stratford East   to
Oxford Circus
Mile End   Woke with impotent bottoms   Pressing   Frantic   To get off

                      Writing for some automatic
Bethnal Green   Geezer with curls   Glasses

Looks with his face at me   Curious with this pen screed I think he missed me
What I'm doing in this book   But nobody else figured it out yet
                                        What I'm doing

New Tube Snake waiting

Writing their stuff in this book

New Tube Woman

She looks at me

Curious with her gold rot beyond the glass

Veins come out of the hole

Automatic glass gone smooth

RED POLES
GREY POLES

FAKE MARBLE
FAKE PONY SKIN MINI
SKIRT

The laughing boys excited
Adjust their trousers
Tottenham Court road
No more alcohol
Jelly fish
Climbing up the hole into the sun

New Tube Woman

MONUMENTAL

Modernism was a combination of the diminutive and the grand. The work presented here reflects the latter, either in terms of media used (environmental graphics that employ large-scale objects, such as banners) or in terms of typographic scale (huge types contrasted with small ones).

FUTU MAGAZINE • A one-off design by Studio8Design for the sixth issue of bilingual (Polish/English) magazine *FUTU*. All Polish text runs in black, while the English text is red. **DESIGN FIRM:** Studio8 Design **DESIGNER:** Matt Willey **CLIENT:** *FUTU* magazine **PUBLISHER:** Publishing and Design Group **PRIMARY FONTS:** Fat Face, Champion, Chaparral

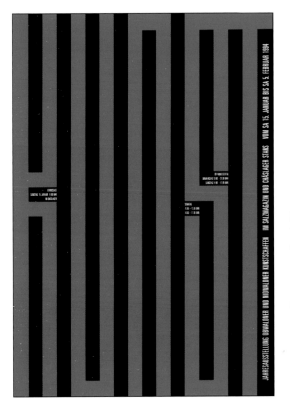

HAPPY TYPOGRAPHIC FAMILIES • This is a happy families game. The goal is to learn, understand, and revise typographic families. The set includes seventy-four 5.8 x 9.3 cm cards in a Plexiglas box. The type is set in French and English and the scale gives it a monumental dimension. **DESIGN FIRM:** Editions/Bureau 205 **ART DIRECTOR:** Damien Gautier **DESIGNERS:** Damien Gautier, Quentin Margat, Delphine Sigonney **CLIENT:** Editions 205 **PRIMARY FONTS:** Helvetica, Knockout, Replica, Colonel, Amiral (and many others from Emigre, Underware, FontFont, 256tm, Linotype, 205, etc.)

KUNST • The influence here is Russian Constructivism. This piece was created for an art exhibition featuring artists of Central Switzerland organized by the Nidwaldner Museum in Stans. **DESIGN FIRM:** Melchior Imboden, Graphic Atelier **ART DIRECTOR AND DESIGNER:** Melchior Imboden **CLIENT:** Nidwaldner Museum, Stans **PRINTER:** Bösch Siebdruck AG, Stans **PRIMARY FONT:** Univers Compressed

MONUMENTAL

170 **THE YEAR IN CULTURE: 2006** • The backwards "six" is a startling bullseye on the front page of the Arts & Leisure supplement in *The New York Times*. Turning it around forces the viewer to ask "why?" **DESIGN FIRM:** Post Typography **ART DIRECTORS AND DESIGNERS:** Nolen Strals, Bruce Willen **CLIENT AND PUBLISHER:** *The New York Times* **PRIMARY FONT:** United Stencil

ROPPONGI HILLS • Design firm Barnbrook created this corporate identity for Roppongi Hills, the largest postwar development in Tokyo. **DESIGN FIRM:** Barnbrook **CREATIVE DIRECTOR:** Scott Dadich **ART DIRECTOR:** Jonathan Barnbrook **DESIGNER:** Jonathan Barnbrook, Marcus Leis Allion, Pedro Inoue **CLIENT:** Roppongi Hills **PRIMARY FONT:** Priori

MONUMENTAL

SOME IDEAS ON LIVING IN LONDON AND TOKYO • Street postering and the functional typography found in urban settings were the main influences for these exhibition graphics. "Some Ideas on Living in London and Tokyo" showed residential architecture projects built in the cities of London (by British architect Stephen Taylor) and Tokyo (by Japanese architect Ryue Nishizawa). A play on scale was created, with some posters containing entire texts, others only titles, and others still massive individual letters. **DESIGN FIRM:** Feed **ART DIRECTORS AND DESIGNERS:** Anouk Pennel, Raphaël Daudelin **PHOTOGRAPHER:** CCA, Montréal Experimental Jetset **CLIENT:** Canadian Centre for Architecture (CCA) **PRIMARY FONTS:** Titling (in a custom font), Eureka Mono

172

SEATTLE INT'L FILM FEST • The Seattle International Film Festival is the largest film festival in North America. For twenty-five days, the festival engulfs the city in a big and exciting way, which warrants the choice of sharp, thunderous type and images. Benjamin K. Shown names Russian Constructivism and Soviet-era propaganda posters as influences, adding "I wanted the type to convey an impending and uneasy magnitude." **DESIGN FIRM:** University of Washington **ART DIRECTOR:** Annabelle Gould **DESIGNER:** Benjamin K. Shown **CLIENT:** Seattle International Film Festival **PRIMARY FONTS:** Red October, Fedra Serif

MONUMENTAL

Below:
Green (Epthalpui)
Paper ephemera collage
52.1 x 19.7 cm
2007

100

ELEPHANT MAGAZINE • In this design work for *Elephant*, a quarterly art and culture magazine, the typography is multidimensional and gives an impression of force and strength. **DESIGN FIRM:** Studio8 Design **DESIGNER:** Matt Willey **CLIENT:** Frame Publishing **PRIMARY FONTS:** Custom, Parry

HOFER WANTED • Words on walls and on banners envelop this exhibition space with various messages and meanings. **DESIGN FIRM:** L2M3 Kommunikationsdesign GmbH (Architecture: büro münzing) **ART DIRECTOR:** Sascha Lobe **DESIGNERS:** Sascha Lobe, Dirk Wachowiak, Sven Thiery **PHOTOGRAPHER:** Brigida González **CLIENT:** Tiroler Landesmuseum, Innsbruck **PRIMARY FONTS:** Conduit ITC, Univers

MONUMENTAL

Studio8 Design: Collaborations in Type & Print

27 May 2010
7pm

The Typographic Circle
JWT, 1 Knightsbridge Green
London SW1X 7NW

www.typocircle.co.uk

Paper by:
GF Smith

Printed on:
GF Smith Colorplan Citrine 170gsm

Printed by:
White Duck Screenprint

STUDIO8 DESIGN: COLLABORATIONS IN TYPE & PRINT • The number eight has an impressive stature in this two-color, A1 screenprinted poster for a lecture given by Studio8 Design at the Typographic Circle. **DESIGN FIRM:** Studio8 Design **DESIGNER:** Matt Willey, Zoë Bather **CLIENT:** The Typographic Circle **PRIMARY FONT:** Freight Sans

FAÇADE DESIGN: KUNSTMUSEUM STUTTGART •
Inspired by the museum's situation in the middle of the city's pedestrian zone, the façade design mimics the mechanisms of commercial window advertising, playing with size and register to give a special interpretation of these familiar advertising symbols. **DESIGN FIRM:** L2M3 Kommunikationsdesign GmbH **ART DIRECTOR:** Sascha Lobe **DESIGNERS:** Sabine Braun, Sascha Lobe, Kathrin Löser, Jan Maier, Gabriele Ruf **CLIENT:** Kunstmuseum Stuttgart **PRIMARY FONT:** Bureau Grotesque

MONUMENTAL

KREISSPARKASSE LUDWIGSBURG • All branches of German bank Kreissparkasse operate independently from one another, so the designers tried to find individual local references for the lettering they created in each building. "The key themes for Ludwigsburg," says Sascha Lobe, "were the Baroque, with its architectural trompe-l'oeils, and a 140m-long access corridor that connects the various sections of the new building." The story and staircase signs "are so distorted in perspective that they can only be viewed correctly from one point and otherwise morph into a game of free forms." **DESIGN FIRM:** L2M3 Kommunikationsdesign GmbH **ART DIRECTOR:** Sascha Lobe **DESIGNERS:** Frank Geiger, Sascha Lobe **CLIENT:** Kreissparkasse Ludwigsburg **PRIMARY FONTS:** Sparkasse, Helvetica

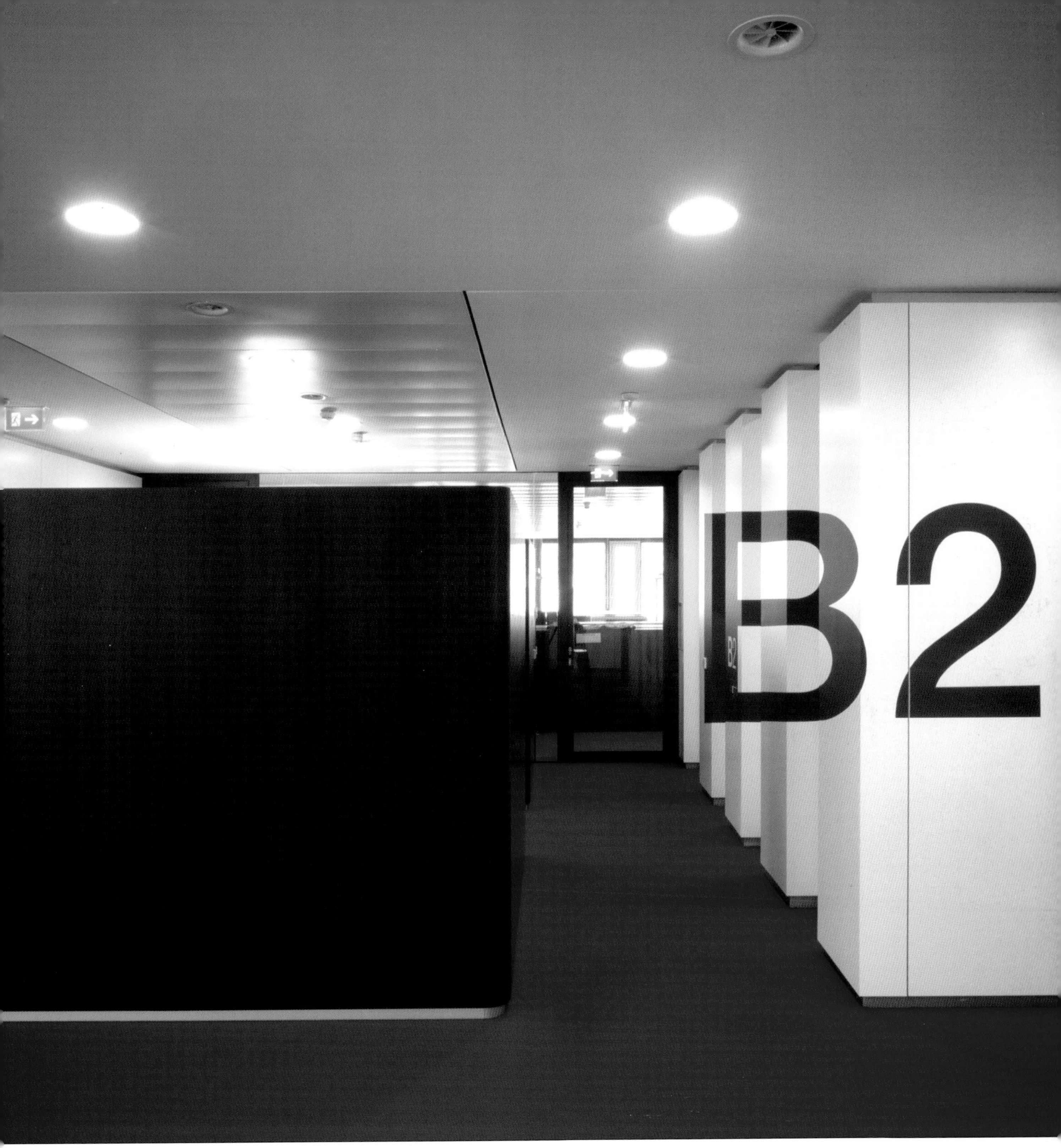
B2

MONUMENTAL

■
■

■
■

DIE SCHÖNSTEN DEUTSCHEN BÜCHER, 2007 • A journey through the German bookscape is the subject of this catalog. "Arranged like a landscape," says Sascha Lobe, "it allows the reader to get a comprehensive impression of the books presented here. Multiple spreads from each book are laid out next to one another, so that the characteristic style of the layout becomes visible, while details are shown in large format. Set pieces from the world of model railways subtly explore the content of the various books featured. The result is a vividness with a sense of wit and irony." **DESIGN FIRM:** L2M3 Kommunikationsdesign GmbH **ART DIRECTOR:** Sascha Lobe **DESIGNERS:** Ina Bauer, Sascha Lobe, Thorsten Steidle **PHOTOGRAPHER:** Wolfram Palmer **PUBLISHER:** Stiftung Buchkunst **PRIMARY FONT:** Akzidenz-Grotesk

623 FIFTH AVENUE •
Pentagram designed the
identity and entry signage
for 623 Fifth Avenue, a
thirty-six-story, limestone-
clad office building in
Midtown Manhattan
purchased by developer
Charles S. Cohen in 2002.
Cohen wanted to give the
building a distinctive identity
by rebranding it with a Fifth
Avenue address, which
would help it stand out
in one of the city's most
competitive markets. For
its 50th-Street entrance,
the designers created a
highly visible entry feature
that establishes a strong,
contemporary identity for
the building. The numbers
on the sign are 10 feet high
and made of brass. At night
these are backlit by the
lights inside the building,
creating a visually dramatic
presence. **DESIGN FIRM:**
Pentagram Design **ART
DIRECTOR:** Paula Scher
PHOTOGRAPHER: Peter
Mauss/Esto **CLIENT:** Cohen
Brothers Realty Corporation
PRIMARY FONT: Agency

181

MONUMENTAL

BLOOMBERG CORPORATE HEADQUARTERS • Pentagram created signage, environmental graphics, and media installations for the new corporate headquarters of Bloomberg, the financial news, data, and analytics provider. Working with Studios Architecture, Pentagram created an interior that seamlessly communicates Bloomberg's brand, products, and services. It includes identification signage for floors, rooms, and elevators; directory signage and wayfinding; and several dynamic, superscale media installations, displaying live content from Bloomberg's own news and data feeds. For the graphics, the designers developed a font called Bloomberg, merging the letters of the font Avenir with the numerals of Avant Garde. In the numbers, an Avant Garde "O" was used instead of a zero to create the impression of Bloomberg-branded data. **DESIGN FIRM:** Pentagram Design **ART DIRECTOR AND DESIGNER:** Paula Scher **PHOTOGRAPHER:** Peter Mauss/Esto **CLIENT:** Bloomberg **PRIMARY FONT:** Bloomberg

MONUMENTAL

BCAD • This book about Dutch architects Benthem Crouwel was produced on the occasion of their 30th anniversary. It evokes a decidedly economical modernist aesthetic; the size and composition of the book cover suggest strength and authority. **DESIGN FIRM:** Studio Laucke **ART DIRECTORS AND DESIGNERS:** Dirk Laucke, Johanna Siebein **CLIENT:** Benthem Crouwel Architects **PUBLISHER:** 010 publisher, Rotterdam **PRIMARY FONTS:** Akzidenz-Grotesk, Futura

184

MANIFESTEZ-VOUS • "In French 'manifestez-vous' means 'express yourself'… So that's what we have done," says Pierre Vanni. "In front of the Centre Pompidou, we built streamers that could be seen by everyone, and I then took a picture." This visual was designed to promote an exhibition curated by the Centre Pompidou that was aimed at teenagers. **DESIGN FIRM:** Pierre Vanni **ART DIRECTOR AND DESIGNER:** Pierre Vanni **CLIENT:** Centre Pompidou **PRIMARY FONT:** DIN

CHEVROLET SUMMER • Chevrolet and McCann Erickson Argentina commissioned Pablo Alfieri to work on the print campaign and the demo of this TV Spot, "Vacaciones Y Auto." Chevrolet had a lot to say and the ads had needed to include much information, so the designer decided to play with the typography, "adding freshness and fun." Alfieri used the Neutra Black font as inspiration.
DESIGN FIRM: Plenty **ART DIRECTOR AND DESIGNER:** Pablo Alfieri **CLIENT:** General Motors
PRIMARY FONT: Neutra Black

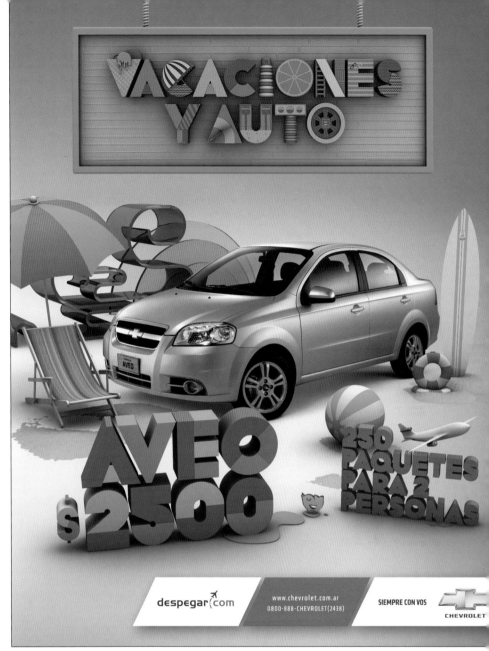

MONUMENTAL

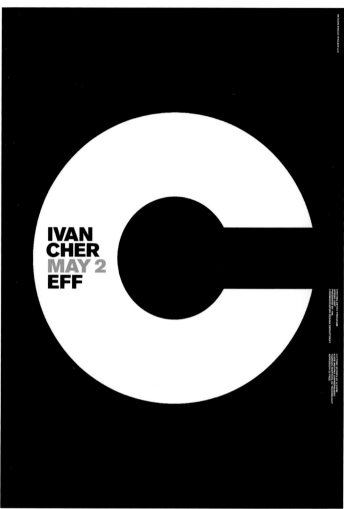

VISITING ARTIST PROGRAM AT FIT • What can be more monumental than a big "c" (or a big "dc")? In this case, the letters announce David Carson and Ivan Chermayeff, the modernists' modern designer. **DESIGN FIRM:** Piscatello Design Centre **DESIGNER:** Rocco Piscatello **CLIENT:** Fashion Institute of Technology **PRIMARY FONTS:** Custom "c," Akzidenz-Grotesk

ELEPHANT MAGAZINE • The use of a slab serif and drop shadows gives dimension and weight to this magazine spread. **DESIGN FIRM:** Studio8 Design **DESIGNER:** Matt Willey **CLIENT:** Frame Publishing **PRIMARY FONTS:** Custom, Parry

EARTHQUAKES

IN

'If you haven't been to Berlin in the Summer, you've never been to Berlin,' KATYA TYLEVICH *is told as she sips Rhineland wine in art and design studios, or sits on sofas in the streets, or fails to find her subjects on the crowded Tiergarten grass, or sits on overcrowded terraces and bars (with vuvuzelas echoing in the background and beer flowing all around) discussing the unique artistic atmosphere of this city.*

PHOTOGRAPHS BY ALEXEI TYLEVICH

RETRO

Modernism is about the present and the future, not the past. And yet, design is impossible without retrospection. Even during the 1920s and 1930s, modernists recalled the past – if only to transform and transmute it. In contemporary design the old is often replayed, either for its nostalgic import or as a stepping stone to the future. The designers here have, for the most part, quoted and sampled from a variety of modernist pasts.

ROBU BOLD • Andrei Robu developed a woodcut-inspired typeface to create a vintage look for titles and posters. **DESIGN FIRM:** Andrei Robu **ART DIRECTOR, DESIGNER, AND ILLUSTRATOR:** Andrei Robu **PRIMARY FONT:** Robu Bold

ABCDEF GHIJKLM NOPQRS TUVWX YZ

abcdef ghijklm nopqr stuvw xyz ?!.,.:;() +-

THE WHOLE MESS

NOVEMBER 2009

GOOD VALUE

FIELD NOTES "THE KIT"

GOOD VALUE

FIELD NOTES

2010
2009 · 2011

18-MONTH WORK STATION CALENDAR

Our Logo:

1 - 3-Pack Graph Paper
1 - 3-Pack Mixed Paper
6 - Clic Pen Ballpoint Pens
6 - No.2 Woodgrain Pencils
1 - 18-Monther Calendar

The whole kit and caboodle. It's gonna be a big year, so get yourself prepared for all the action with "THE KIT" from FIELD NOTES.

ADD TO CART

ACT NOW........$34.95

FIELD NOTES
Graph Paper

FIELD NOTES
Mixed Three-Pack

THE KIT (FIELD NOTES) • The influences for Field Notes notebooks are old equipment manuals and other forgotten pieces of American utilitarian design. "Why buy only one memo book when you can go for broke and stock up? Hence 'The Kit'," says designer Aaron James Draplin. **DESIGN FIRM:** Draplin Design Co. **ART DIRECTOR:** Jim Coudal (Coudal Partners) **DESIGNERS:** Bryan Bedell, Aaron James Draplin **ILLUSTRATOR:** Aaron James Draplin **PHOTOGRAPHER:** Bryan Bedell **CLIENT:** Field Notes **PRIMARY FONT:** Futura Bold

EDITED BY
ELISABETH S. CLEMENS
AND
DOUG GUTHRIE

POLITICS **+**
PARTNERSHIPS

**THE ROLE OF
VOLUNTARY ASSOCIATIONS
IN AMERICA'S POLITICAL
PAST AND PRESENT**

POLITICS + PARTNERSHIPS ▪
This book is a collection of academic
essays on the history of the relationship
between volunteer organizations and
the U.S. government. The styles of the
WPA (Works Progress Administration)
and Lester Beall are overtly invoked
in the design of the book's cover.
DESIGN FIRM: The University of
Chicago Press **ART DIRECTOR:** Jill
Shimabukuro **DESIGNER:** Isaac Tobin
PHOTOGRAPHER: Library of Congress
(Picture Archive) **PUBLISHER:** The
University of Chicago Press **PRIMARY
FONTS:** Public Gothic, Gotham

RETRO

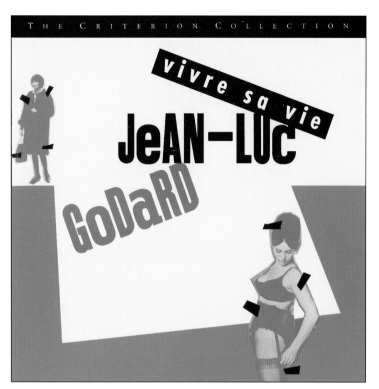

VIVRE SA VIE (JEAN-LUC GODARD) • "I was thinking about Lester Beall's work when designing this," Koppel explains. "I actually started to think: 'What if Lester Beall was given an Elvis Costello CD to design?' This was my approach, but I know he would have done a better design." **DESIGN FIRM:** T. Koppel Design **ART DIRECTOR AND DESIGNER:** Terry Koppel **PHOTOGRAPHER:** Theatrical Publicity Photos/Movie Stills **CLIENT:** The Criterion Collection **PRIMARY FONTS:** Eseventeen, WoodBlockCond, Luxor, ETen, ETwentyFive

THE RED CABBAGE CAFÉ • Influenced by Soviet film posters, this design for a book cover seems to involve a mysterious woman, a bear, and a recording by Lenin. **DESIGN FIRM:** Archie Ferguson Design **ART DIRECTOR:** Marjorie Anderson **DESIGNER AND ILLUSTRATOR:** Archie Ferguson **CLIENT:** Pantheon Books **PRIMARY FONTS:** Handset and altered, xeroxed type from vintage type books

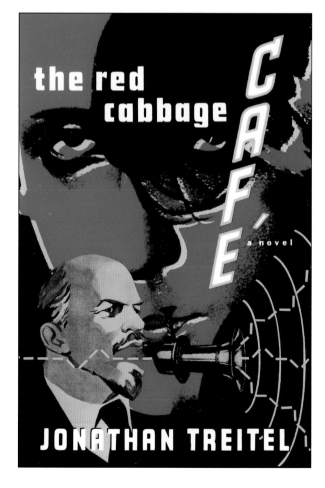

TROCHUT (Bold)

ABCDEFGHIJKLMNOPQRSTUVWXYZ
abcdefghijklmnopqrstuvwxyz

0123456789 #%‰ $¢£€¥ Ww çñàáâãäåèéêëìíîïòóôõöœùúûüÿ ↑↓§¶ fifl ß@
¡¿?!()[]\{}«»‹›/·-/-—_''""„'‚‹›•*‚""@©™-{}· ¸çñàáâãäåèéêëìíîïòóôõöœùúûüÿ .,:;

Mix Zapf with Veljovic and get quirky Beziers

Lorem ipsum dolor sit amet, consectetuer adipiscing elit. Etiam mi dolor, interdum ac, ornare in, interdum et, velit. Nulla eget nunc a odio vestibulum iaculis. Phasellus ullamcorper. In dictum, odio in vestibulum pellentesque, diam ante imperdiet velit, eu dapibus leo dui eu dolor. Aenean pretium, dui eu ultricies mattis, nisl ipsum venenatis nulla, non egestas diam tellus quis ante. Nunc porta sempre elit. Maecenas sed elit. Morbi auctor, quam eget elementum consectetuer, nibh purus vestibulum turpis, non interdum nunc dolor in ligula. Aenean sit amet augue. Vivamus elementum luctus tellus. In urna turpis, semper eget,

consequat et, eleifend in, mauris. Nulla fringilla wisi ut lectus. Duis sed velit. Curabitur pharetra sollicitudin ipsum. Donec orci justo, facilisis non, tristique tincidunt, blandit ut, urna. Nam ullamcorper bibendum metus. Sed imperdiet. Suspendisse potenti. Duis aliquet commodo sapien. Phasellus semper, ipsum et pharetra consectetuer, nunc libera pretium mauris, sit amet posuere nisl libero ac quam. Vestibulum pulvinar. Aenean et nisl. Quisque sem. Nam laoreet tincidunt nibh. Pellentesque odio velit, tempor et, volutpat sit amet, euismod at, risus. Ut vitae ante. Nunc sit amet turpis. Integer tempor porttitor in-

A.C. DOCUMENTS D'ACTIVITAT CONTEMPORÀNIA

monaco grand prix
visca la república!

COOL GIRLS
VODKA

TROCHUT (the homage family) by Andreu Balius, is greatly inspired on the typeface design of catalan type designer & printer Joan Trochut Blanchart !

TROCHUT (Regular)

ABCDEFGHIJKLMNOPQRSTUVWXYZ
abcdefghijklmnopqrstuvwxyz

0123456789 #%‰ $¢£€¥ Ww çñàáâãäåèéêëìíîïòóôõöœùúûüÿ ↑↓§¶ fifl ß@
¡¿?!()[]\{}«»‹›/·-/-—_''""„'‚‹›•*‚""@©™-{}· ¸çñàáâãäåèéêëìíîïòóôõöœùúûüÿ .,:;

That quick brown dog jumped over the lazy fox

Lorem ipsum dolor sit amet, consectetuer adipiscing elit. Etiam mi dolor, interdum ac, ornare in, interdum et, velit. Nulla eget nunc a odio vestibulum iaculis. Phasellus ullamcorper. In dictum, odio in vestibulum pellentesque, diam ante imperdiet velit, eu dapibus leo dui eu dolor. Aenean pretium, dui eu ultricies mattis, nisl ipsum venenatis nulla, non egestas diam tellus quis ante. Nunc porta sempre elit. Maecenas sed elit. Morbi auctor, quam eget elementum consectetuer, nibh purus vestibulum turpis, non interdum nunc dolor in ligula. Aenean sit amet augue. Vivamus elementum luctus tellus. In urna turpis, semper eget, consequat et, eleifend in, mau-ris. Nulla fringilla wisi ut lectus. Duis sed velit. Curabitur pharetra sollici-

tudin ipsum. Donec orci justo, facilisis non, tristique tincidunt, blandit ut, urna. Nam ullamcorper bibendum metus. Sed imperdiet. Suspendisse potenti. Duis aliquet commodo sapien. Phasellus semper, ipsum et pharetra consectetuer, nunc libera pretium mauris, sit amet posuere nisl libero ac quam. Vestibulum pulvinar. Aenean et nisl. Quisque sem. Nam laoreet tincidunt nibh. Pellentesque odio velit, tempor et, volutpat sit amet, euismod at, risus. Ut placerat, augue id ornare blandit, tortor erat auctor do-

HUMPHREY BOGART AUDREY HEPBURN & WILLIAM HOLDEN

sanremo capri roma
venezia & isla bonita

bossa nova
SITGES

TROCHUT (the homage family) by Andreu Balius, is greatly inspired on the typeface design of catalan type designer & printer Joan Trochut Blanchart !

TROCHUT TYPEFACE • Trochut is designed as an interpretation of the Bisonte typeface, which was designed by Joan Trochut in the 1940s and quite obviously inspired by the modern spirit of those years. **DESIGN FIRM AND DESIGNER:** Andreu Balius **CLIENT:** Typerepublic **PRIMARY FONT:** Trochut

TROCHUT
Andreu Balius (2003)

TOUR DE FRANCE
Paris/Tolouse/Sant Hilari/Cantonigrós/Lleida

L'aplec del Cargol

Gran Hotel

BARCELONA

LOS MODERNOS ALMACENES

sepu

Calçotets, Barretines, Faixes, Bates,   Samarretes, Mitges i Corbates

¡en ofertas navideñas!

RETRO

CALIFORNICATION!

A NEW SCREWBALL COMEDY STARRING ARNOLD SCHWARZENEGGER, GARY COLEMAN, ARIANNA HUFFINGTON, LARRY FLYNT AND THE MOST BORING WHITE MAN IN AMERICA, GRAY DAVIS. YOU'LL LAUGH. YOU'LL CRY. YOU'LL WONDER IF POLITICS WILL EVER BE THE SAME
BY LISA DePAULO

ON A TUESDAY NIGHT in mid-August, after the worst week of any living politician's life—with the exception of Bill, but at least he got sex out of it—Gray Davis agrees to a meeting. He's holed up in his L.A. bunker, a cluttered rented spread on Pico Boulevard that serves as headquarters for "Californians Against the *Costly* Recall," as his staff is now forced to answer the phones, where every piece of furniture is temporary—including, perhaps, the governor—and where the air-conditioning snaps off at 5 p.m. but the governor does not. No, sirree, he will *stay here and sweat*, late into the night, won't even loosen that noose of a necktie—clearly, the man has not been tortured enough—all in the service of the good people of California, who, in the next poll, will claim that they hate him every bit as much as Richard Nixon. >>>

OCTOBER 2003 **GQ** 219

CALIFORNICATION • Although this *GQ* spread clearly shows Arnold Schwarzenegger, the graphic conceit derives from another era – namely, WPA, Lester Beall, and Leo Lionni posters of the late 1930s and early 1940s. **DESIGN DIRECTOR:** Fred Woodward **DESIGNER:** Ken DeLago **CLIENT:** *GQ* **PUBLISHER:** Condé Nast **PRIMARY FONT:** Replica

THE EAMES EXPERIENCE · This is the opening spread of a breakthrough story for *Metropolis* in which Lucia Eames (daughter of Charles Eames) showed the designers each part of the family's iconic modern home and talked about what it was like to grow up in a home revered by modern architects and designers. The layout reflects both that experience and the Eames style. **DESIGN FIRM:** *Metropolis* magazine **ART DIRECTORS:** Criswell Lappin, Nancy Nowacek **PHOTOGRAPHER:** Misha Gravenor **PUBLISHER:** Bellerophon Publishers **PRIMARY FONT:** Robust ICG

BASQUIAT · "Basquiat is one of my favorite artists," says Bonnie Clas, "and I loved this quote of his. The ideas of royalty, youth, and decadence led me to explore creating letterforms that looked like bent and glittering pieces of gold. Each letter has several layers of digital coloring and custom brushes to really achieve the effect." The type suggests the art deco aesthetic. **DESIGNER AND ILLUSTRATOR:** Bonnie Clas **PRIMARY FONT:** Custom lettering

RETRO

MONDO CANE • "This poster and direct mail piece announcing a move to a new store location is slightly influenced by Paul Rand," Terry Koppel notes. **DESIGN FIRM:** T. Koppel Design **ART DIRECTOR AND DESIGNER:** Terry Koppel **PHOTOGRAPHER:** Patrick Parrish **CLIENT:** Mondo Cane **PRIMARY FONTS:** Grotesque Bold, Bodoni Italic

194

JOHNSON'S BACKYARD GARDEN CSA (COMMUNITY SUPPORTED AGRICULTURE) BOX • Quilts, plots of land, dirt, back to basics, simple life, stamps, and folk art are all influences for this piece. "Brenton Johnson asked me to rebrand his farm," says designer Ryan Rhodes. "We chose to keep it basic to keep costs down, showcase the natural beauty of the organic veggies, and reflect the homegrown spirit of the farm. The art also allows for constant flexibility as the farm is a living, growing, and continually changing entity." **DESIGN FIRM:** Bigger Than Giants **DESIGNER:** Ryan Rhodes **CLIENT:** Johnson's Backyard Garden **PRIMARY FONT:** Custom

RED CAVALRY • One of the great masterpieces of Russian literature, *Red Cavalry* made the reputation of Isaac Babel, who was killed by Stalin's secret police in 1940. The image used here is taken from a Bolshevik poster. **DESIGN FIRM:** Archie Ferguson Design **ART DIRECTOR:** Ingsu Liu **DESIGNER:** Archie Ferguson **ILLUSTRATOR:** David King Collection, London **CLIENT:** W.W. Norton **PRIMARY FONT:** Agency Gothic Bold

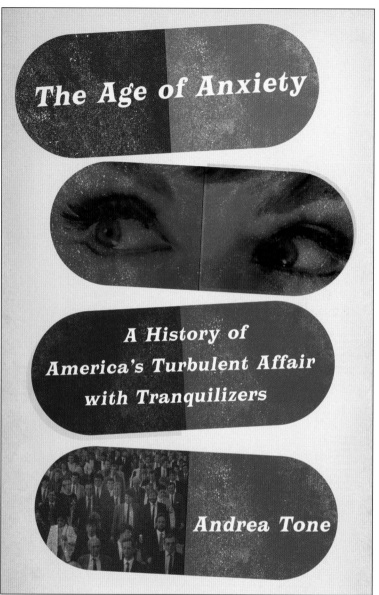

THE AGE OF ANXIETY • The cover of this book, which deals with America's attempts to seek synthetic solutions to everyday angst, was inspired by 1950s public information posters. There is also a hint of Paul Rand's paperback covers. **DESIGN FIRM:** Keenan **ART DIRECTOR:** Nicole Caputo **DESIGNER:** Jamie Keenan **PHOTOGRAPHER:** Getty Images **PUBLISHER:** Basic Books **PRIMARY FONT:** Latin Bold

RETRO

EXAMPLES

THIN EXTRALIGHT LIGHT **REGULAR** MEDIUM **BOLD FAT**

SOME WORDS IN DIFFERENT SIZES & STYLES

ROYAL EXPRESS 1930

DARJEELING

HIMALAYAN RAILWAY

WWW·LETTERWERK·CH | WWW·MYFONTS·COM

COMPANY

IMPERIAL RESIDENZ

BOARDING AT PLATTFORM 2

JASPER NATIONAL PARK

PORT MOODY CANADA

MOMBASA – NAIROBI | MOMBASA – NAIROBI | MOMBASA – NAIROBI

LUXUS TRAIN

PALACE ON WHEELS

CARROSSERIE MEDIUM & CARROSSERIE THIN

ZÜRICH-BERLIN

1 DARJEELING TEE & **3 ESPRESSI ITALIANI**

ORIENTAL LUXUS-LINER ! RETRO TYPE EINE SCHÖNE WANDERUNG NATIONAL PARK
MONTENEGRO FAHRZEUG (KENYA-SAFARI) VANCOUVER TRIP SAFARI @ COMPANION
PASSAGIER KONDUKTEUR-KONTROLLE EISCRÈME →GOOD LUCK! DELHI BAZAAR NAIROBI
WWW·DOMAIN·COM EXOTIC LANDSCAPES! ISTANBUL GLÜCK KOMMT OFT ÜBERRASCHEND
BILLET OUI -LE-GARÇON **CARROSSERIE** BAR &*
POSTCARD CAPE VERDE THE BELLE VOYAGE 1930 NORTH BRITISH COMPANY PALACE ON WHEELS CAFÉ SEATTLE
«SILIGURI BOILS THE CURRY» CALCUTTA MADE FOR **DISPLAY USE** € DELUX
MOVIE THEATER & ROYAL EUROPA PARIS KAKAOBOHNE BEST PRICE! ↦ MANUFACTURER NO. 1270 ·CH· CAPS...
CAPPUCCINO CUP BOARDING AT: PLATTFORM 1 EXPRESS CÔTE D'AZURE | DARJEELING TEA JANUAR LETTERWERK FRIEND

◇ CHARACTER SET ◇

ABCDEFGHIJKLMNOPQRSTUVWXYZ | 0123456789

.,:;!?...----—/+-=<>(){}[|]%«»""''& | €¢$£¥ | ◇@§*

ÑÇÉÎÒÜÅß | ¼½¾⅓¼⅓½⅔ | ©®

· ALTERNATE GLYPHS ·

AAEFJMQ | 1 | & & | ↤·↦ ←*→

◇ DOMAIN GLYPHS ◇

WWW·DOMAIN·COM

·CH··DE··LI··NL··FR··AT··UK··ES··ORG··EU··IT··CA··US·

CARROSSERIE • Typeface Carrosserie (French for "car body") is made for display use and was inspired by the shapes of the 1930s. Carrosserie is a capital-letter font with alternate lettershapes you can play around with, such as an "A" with rounded top or an "M" with thin legs. There are some great alternate ampersands for creating company logos. The font with its vintage shapes can also be radically updated to the internet age by adding a set of "www." domain symbols. **DESIGN FIRM:** Letterwerk **DESIGNER:** Fabian Widmer **PRIMARY FONT:** Carrosserie

HOWL • Alvin Lustig's book covers influenced this movie poster for an Allen Ginsberg biopic starring James Franco. The design evokes the beatnik, modernist 1950s. **DESIGN FIRM:** Isaac Tobin **ART DIRECTOR:** Zoe Chan **DESIGNER AND ILLUSTRATOR:** Isaac Tobin **CLIENT:** Oscilloscope Laboratories **PUBLISHER:** The University of Chicago Press **PRIMARY FONTS:** Futura Bold, Bauer Bodoni, script lettering by Lauren Nassef

GIRL MEETS PEARL • Vintage
champagne posters from 1920s and
1930s Paris inform this in-store poster
for a skin luminizer that creates a pearl-
like "champagne" glow. **DESIGN FIRM:**
Wink **ART DIRECTORS:** Richard Boynton,
Scott Thares **DESIGNER:** Richard Boynton
ILLUSTRATOR: Eric Cash **CLIENT:** Benefit
Cosmetics **PRIMARY FONTS:** Trade Gothic,
Trade Gothic Extended, Handlettered

STEELWORK • WOODWORK

KARTWHEEL

DAVID CLARK
CRAFTSMAN / MAKER

(512) 820-1518
DAVIDCLARK4@MAC.COM

STRUCTURE • FURNITURE

KARTWHEEL BUSINESS CARD • David Clark asked Ryan Rhodes for a simple identity to brand his custom wood- and steelwork. The mark can be transformed into stamps, a wood-burned brand, and many other makers' marks. The designer's influences are early American type founders. **DESIGN FIRM:** Bigger Than Giants **DESIGNER:** Ryan Rhodes **CLIENT:** David Clark/Kartwheel **PRIMARY FONT:** Custom

NOBODY'S PERFECT • As the book's title directly quotes the last line of the film *Some Like It Hot*, designer Megan Wilson used the typography from the poster of that film. The book is a collection of Anthony Lane's film reviews and essays for *The New Yorker*. "Although the writing is primarily about film, Lane covers many different subjects within that genre so a typographical approach seemed best. The title begged to be presented as a reference to the film *Some Like It Hot*," says Wilson, "which fortunately used very distinctive and irresistible type. The blocks of color were a nod to the film posters of Saul Bass." **ART DIRECTOR:** John Gall **DESIGNER:** Megan Wilson **PUBLISHER:** Vintage Books **PRIMARY FONT:** Handlettered

ANTHONY LANE

NOBODY'S PERFECT

WRITINGS FROM *THE NEW YORKER*

"Lane writes prose the way Fred Astaire danced; his sentences and paragraphs are a sublime, rhythmic concoction of glide and snap, lightness and sting."
—*The New York Times Book Review*

200

VIVA LA BICICLETA • The vintage velodrome image comes to play here. Other influences include Dada, J.R. Kenna of the Bay City Wheelmen, and the photography of George Grantham Bain. **DESIGN FIRM:** Bigger Than Giants **DESIGNER:** Ryan Rhodes **CLIENT:** Viva la Bicicleta **PRIMARY FONTS:** Custom (based on OptiMorgan Five Nine), Garage Gothic

Believe it: Bullet trains are coming. After decades of false starts, planners are finally beginning to make headway on what could become the largest, most complicated infrastructure project ever attempted in the US. The Obama administration got on board with an $8 billion infusion, and more cash is likely en route from Congress. It's enough for Florida and Texas to dust off some previously abandoned plans and for urban clusters in the Northeast and Midwest to pursue some long-overdue upgrades. The nation's test bed will almost certainly be California, which already has voter-approved funding and planning under way. But getting up to speed requires more than just seed money. For trains to beat planes and automobiles, the hardware needs to really fly. Officials are pushing to deploy state-of-the-art rail rockets. Next stop: the future.

AMERICAN

EXPRESS

by James Glave and Rachel Swaby | illustrations by Paul Rogers

201

AMERICAN EXPRESS • The artwork evokes the London Railway posters of the 1920s and 1930s, brought up to date with the introduction of a bullet train. **DESIGN FIRM:** *Wired* magazine **CREATIVE DIRECTOR:** Scott Dadich **DESIGN DIRECTOR:** Wyatt Mitchell **DESIGNER:** Margaret Stuart **PUBLISHER:** Condé Nast **PRIMARY FONT:** Luggage

RETRO

THE FARMER IN THE DELI • This design scheme is reminiscent of the 1950s. It combines a generic product label with a down-home trade character. **DESIGN FIRM:** Wink **ART DIRECTORS:** Richard Boynton, Scott Thares **DESIGNER/ILLUSTRATOR:** Richard Boynton **CLIENT:** The Farmer in the Deli **PRIMARY FONTS:** Compacta, Futura, Clarendon, Vintage Typewriter, Handlettered

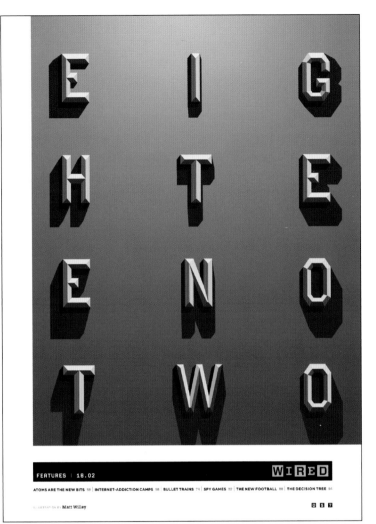

SPLASH PAGE FOR WIRED MAGAZINE • A typographic splash page for the February 2010 issue of *Wired* magazine. **DESIGN FIRM:** Studio8 Design **ART DIRECTOR:** Scott Dadich **DESIGNER:** Matt Willey **CLIENT:** *Wired* magazine **PUBLISHER:** Condé Nast **PRIMARY FONT:** Custom

ADLAND • Television test patterns and television static are the dominating influences in this book cover proposal for a memoir written by a former advertising executive. In the book, Othmer experiences multiple personal and professional crises as he vainly struggles to convince stubborn clients to embrace new and innovative means of promoting their brands. **DESIGN FIRM:** Matt Dorfman/Metalmother **ART DIRECTOR:** John Gall **DESIGNER:** Matt Dorfman **PHOTOGRAPHER:** Corbis/Getty/Veer (Stock) **CLIENT:** Anchor Books **PRIMARY FONTS:** Alternate Gothic, DIN

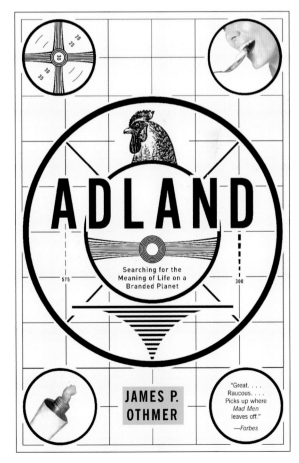

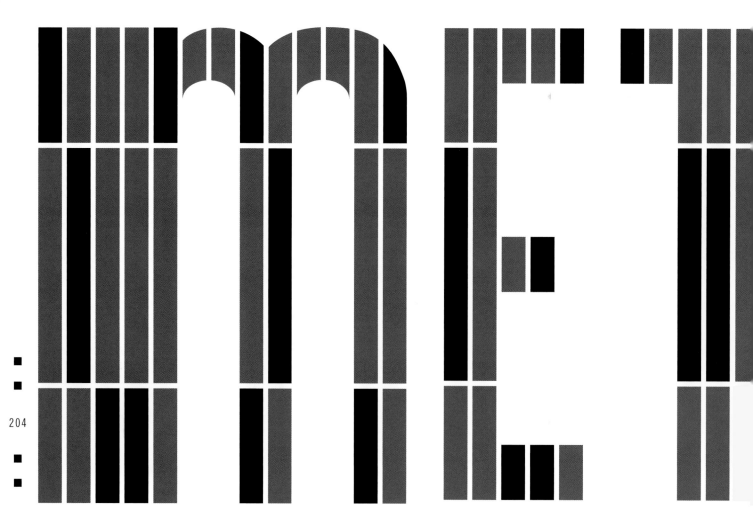

MODERN TYPE IS TYPIFIED by its simplicity and functionality. That is the holy grail of modernism. And in the post-postmodern era, the period that followed an over-abundance of grungy and expressionistic typographies in which typographic rules were flagrantly disregarded as mere fashions, a return to some of those modern truths was to be expected. But even during periods of revival, there can never be an exact return to what came before. Just as digital recordings can never entirely replicate the quirks of analog ones, new/old type is produced in an environment and with technology that produce different – indeed purer – results. So why bother trying to faithfully replicate the old?

Meta modern is not simply modern type cloned and reborn, but rather reappreciated as the basis for something new. Using fundamental modern details as starting points, meta modern takes modernism to another level of impurity. It uses today's computers and other digital drafting tools to make geometrical and optical typographic pyrotechnics. It is also about transforming neutral type into metaphorical icons and symbols.

Starting with a classically modern premise – that type must serve the message, and not be the message – meta modern is a unique, contemporary way of viewing functionality. Modern type is no longer to be viewed through the lens of convention but rather through a more enterprising viewfinder. This means that type can be illustrative or symbolic of the message in addition to being a frame. It can take on a role that is more active than passive. It can impart or imply new things.

This section is about three strands of typographic eclecticism: Optical (presented in a pyrotechnical manner), Geometric (emphasizing the mathematical, even sculptural, qualities of letters), and Metaphorical (standing for something other than what it appears to be).

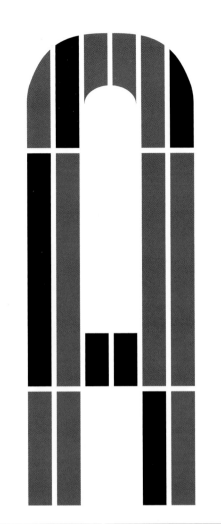

A

MODERN

TYPOGRAPHY
AS
ICON
AND
SYMBOL

GEOMETRIC

The modern typographic ethos was rooted in pure geometry. Futura, the "typeface of the future," was spotlighted for its pure geometric – or vividly mechanical – aesthetic. Paul Rand was once asked whether modernism would ever become old-fashioned. "How can geometry be old-fashioned?", he replied. The work presented here uses geometric forms in pure and "impure" (or eclectic) ways.

Nancy's Closet

PORTRAIT BY **JACKIE NICKERSON**
As first lady, Nancy Reagan was both lauded and lambasted for her lavish,
designer-donated wardrobe. Now 86—but, as she proves, still steely beneath
her diplomat's demeanor—she is putting those glamorous
Galanos gowns and neat Adolfo suits on display.
BY **KEVIN WEST**

Nancy Reagan in
her signature hue

336 | W OCTOBER 2007

206

NANCY'S CLOSET • The dynamic simplicity of the kinetic circles used as a frame for the headline suggests an optical aesthetic. **DESIGN FIRM:** *W* magazine **ART DIRECTOR AND DESIGNER:** Nathalie Kirsheh **PHOTOGRAPHER:** Jackie Nickerson **PUBLISHER:** Condé Nast **PRIMARY FONT:** June

KIELER WOCHE • The famous *Gastrotypographicalassemblage* by Lou Dorfsman (lettering by Herb Lubalin and Tom Carnase, 1966), which hung in the cafeteria of the CBS headquarters in New York, was "a direct influence," says Andrea Tinnes. The Kieler Woche (Kiel Week) is an annual event in the city of Kiel, in northern Germany. It is one of the largest summer festivals in northern Europe and the largest sailing event in the world. The main idea of the poster was to focus on the international character of the festival, expressed through language (verbal and visual). **DESIGNER:** Andrea Tinnes **CLIENT:** Kieler-Woche-Büro **PRIMARY FONTS:** Kieler Woche custom symbol font, Univers, Arial Unicode MS

WHO THE HELL IS ANGELA DAVIS? • This is a promotional poster for an event held at the Maryland Institute College of Art. It was printed as two-color silkscreen on off-white paper. Oliver Munday notes his influences were "Barbara Kruger and Max Huber." **DESIGN FIRM:** Oliver Munday Group (OMG) **DESIGNER:** Oliver Munday **CLIENT:** Maryland Institute College of Art **PRIMARY FONT:** Futura

GEOMETRIC

CAMUS PAPERBACK SERIES • This series redesign of the complete works of Albert Camus recalls the posters of Armin Hofmann. And yet, the designer explains, "there isn't a specific reference for this series, at least not one I'm consciously aware of. It is a combination of a few different things that together reference the modernist era." **ART DIRECTOR:** John Gall **DESIGNER AND ILLUSTRATOR:** Helen Yentus **CLIENT:** Vintage Books **PRIMARY FONTS:** Century, Akzidenz-Grotesk

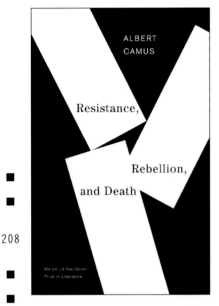

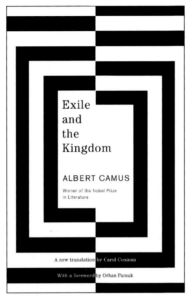

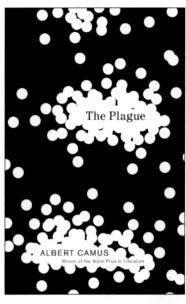

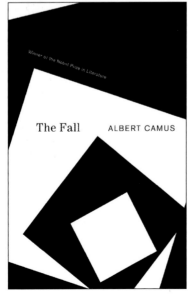

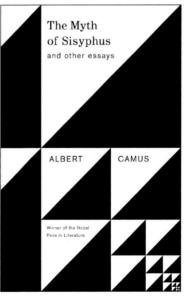

CROSSING THE DIVIDE • Kelly Blair employs the decidedly modern graphic technique of the organizational chart, which came to prominence during the early 20th century, brightened up with colored circles. **DESIGN FIRM:** Kelly Blair Design **ART DIRECTOR:** Stephani Finks **DESIGNER:** Kelly Blair **PUBLISHER:** Harvard Business Review Press **PRIMARY FONT:** Interstate

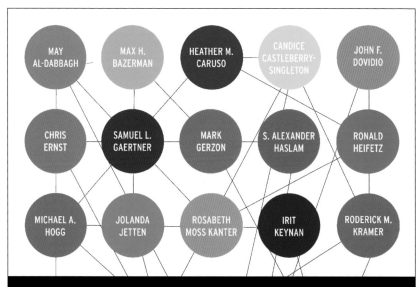

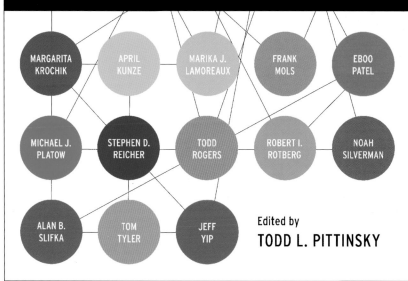

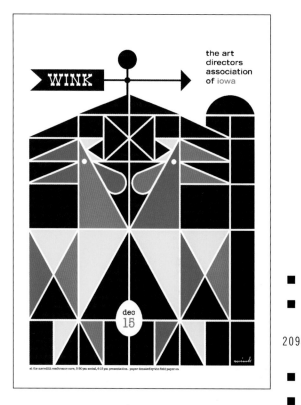

ADAI POSTER • Based on the Streamline and art deco posters created for the 1930s WPA (Works Progress Administration), this poster announces a lecture by Richard Boynton and Scott Thares of Wink. **DESIGN FIRM:** Wink **ART DIRECTORS, DESIGNERS, AND ILLUSTRATORS:** Richard Boynton, Scott Thares **CLIENT:** Art Directors Association of Iowa **PRIMARY FONTS:** Trade Gothic Extended, American Typewriter, Handlettered

GEOMETRIC

THE WALLFLOWERS • Poster for The Wallflowers' 2009 concert in Columbus, Ohio. The idea was to create a bold and graphic type solution so Base Art Co. started with a cubic grid and began building letterforms **DESIGN FIRM:** Base Art Co. **ART DIRECTOR:** Terry Rohrbach **DESIGNERS:** Terry Rohrbach, Drue Dixon **CLIENT:** PromoWest Productions **PRIMARY FONTS:** Self-generated modular lettering based on a cubic grid, Knockout

RENEE RHYNER & CO • This logo design for artist agency Renee Rhyner & Co. references Renee's personal taste and distinct details from around her home, where she has surrounded herself with inspiring artworks and flowering gardens. **DESIGN FIRM:** TBA+D **DESIGNER:** Tom Brown (TBA+D) **CLIENT:** Renee Rhyner & Co. **PRIMARY FONT:** Avant Garde ITC

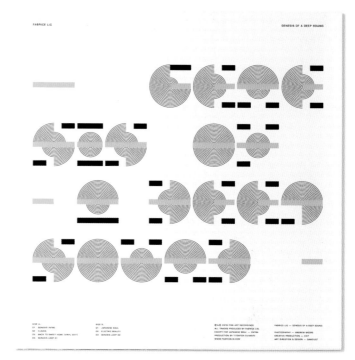

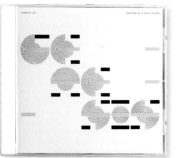

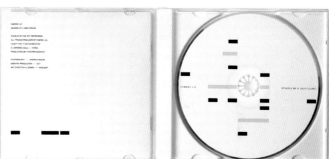

FABRICE LIG – GENESIS OF A DEEP SOUND • This album artwork for CD and vinyl reveals a unique personal alphabetical vocabulary made from geometric elements. **DESIGN FIRM:** Sawdust **ART DIRECTORS AND DESIGNERS:** Jonathan Quainton, Rob Gonzalez **PHOTOGRAPHER:** Andrew Moore **CLIENT:** Fine Art Recordings **PRIMARY FONT:** Custom typography

COLLINS • This identity design for Collins was inspired by the colon. "Of all the punctuation marks, the colon is arguably the most social," Brian Collins explains. "It pulls us deeper into the text, introducing new ideas, new details, and new story elements." **DESIGN FIRM:** Collins **EXECUTIVE CREATIVE DIRECTOR:** Brian Collins **CREATIVE DIRECTOR:** John Fulbrook III **SENIOR DESIGN DIRECTOR:** Kevin Brainard **DESIGNERS:** Kevin Brainard, John Fulbrook III **PRIMARY FONT:** Collins Geometric (drawn by James Montalbano, Terminal Design)

GEOMETRIC

FEIST • These bird shapes came from a study of simple patterns. The result is a very mid-century-modern look. **DESIGN FIRM:** Dan Stiles **ART DIRECTOR, DESIGNER, AND ILLUSTRATOR:** Dan Stiles **CLIENT:** Monqui Presents **PRIMARY FONTS:** Futura Book, Chalet LondonNineteenEighty

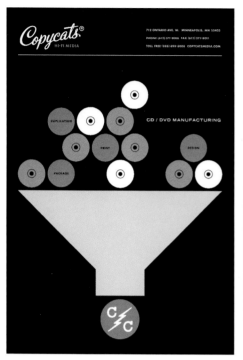
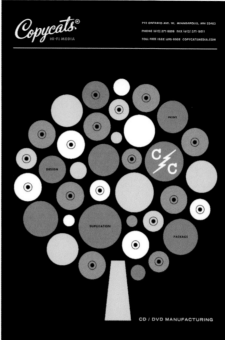
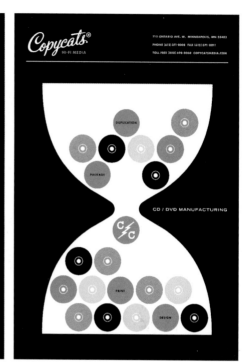

COPYCATS • These three color posters for a CD and DVD manufacturer were influenced by 1960s manufacturing ads and annual report information graphics. **DESIGN FIRM:** Wink **ART DIRECTORS:** Richard Boynton, Scott Thares **DESIGNER AND ILLUSTRATOR:** Richard Boynton **CLIENT:** Copycats **PRIMARY FONTS:** Futura Bold, Trade Gothic Extended, Handlettered

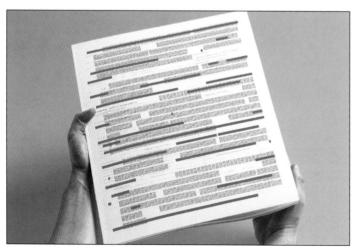

CROSSROADS VERSUS ROUNDABOUTS • This catalog, which accompanied Leszek Knaflewski's "Crossroads versus Roundabouts" exhibition at Galeria Piekary in Poland, was inspired by cryptographic and encryption algorithms. The cover was printed in CMYK on 350 g/m² cardboard with pearl laminate and Spot UV ink. **DESIGN FIRM:** 3group **ART DIRECTOR AND DESIGNER:** Ryszard Bienert **PHOTOGRAPHER:** Andrzej Grabowski **CLIENT AND PUBLISHER:** Galeria Piekary **PRIMARY FONTS:** Prestige Elite PL, Orator

GEOMETRIC

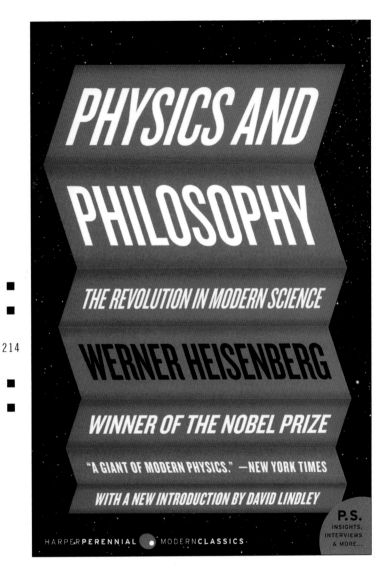

PHYSICS AND PHILOSOPHY • *Physics and Philosophy* is an extremely complicated book, says Gregg Kulick, "unless you have considerable prior knowledge of quantum mechanics, which I do not have. That being said, I do have some basic knowledge of quantum theory and I tried to do an all-type jacket that somehow represented it. To put it simply, quantum physics describes the wave-like behavior of matter so I decided to create a purely typographic design that represents a wave in space."
ART DIRECTOR: Robin Bilardello **DESIGNER:** Gregg Kulick
PUBLISHER: Harper Perennial **PRIMARY FONT:** Knockout

MERCAT DEL GUST • This poster for the "Taste Market," a fair where one can find every kind of foodstuff that comes from the cultivation of the earth, combines two elements: the earth and food. Both are shown with the most elementary symbol, a circle, symbolizing the plate, the earth, and food.
DESIGN FIRM: Bisgrafic **ART DIRECTOR AND DESIGNER:** Bisgrafic **CLIENT:** Council of Vic, Spain **PRIMARY FONT:** Helvetica

BRASILIA • Fifty designers were asked to pay homage to the city of Brasilia and the legacy of modernist Brazilian architect Oscar Niemeyer. The poster here is design firm Tomato's take on this theme. **DESIGN FIRM:** Tomato **DESIGNER:** Dylan Kendle, Simon Taylor **CLIENT:** Brasilia Prima **PRIMARY FONT:** Handlettered

JOURNEYS OF SAPA INCA • Commissioned to design an identity and posters for a series of five lectures by pre-eminent art historians, David Wolske "conceived a set of limited-edition letterpress broadsides printed from handset metal and wood types." "The influences here," Wolske says, "are Inca architecture, ceramics, and textiles. I was also inspired by International Typographic Style, and modern and late-modern poster design. This is the fourth poster in the series." **ART DIRECTOR, DESIGNER, AND ILLUSTRATOR:** David Wolske **CLIENT:** Indiana University (School of Fine Arts) **PRIMARY FONTS:** Univers, 19th-century Gothic woodtype

GEOMETRIC

JUDAH • "The idea behind this font," Bonnie Clas notes, "was to explore and emphasize contrasts between solid, heavy shapes and very thin lines. The idea of reconfiguring counters (as in the "M" and the "N") and the crossbar of the "A" would probably be considered blasphemous to some in terms of legibility – hence the name ('Judah') and the Gustave Doré engraving in the background of the poster." **DESIGNER AND ILLUSTRATOR:** Bonnie Clas **PRIMARY FONT:** Custom lettering

GETTING UPPER • For its 2011 "Getting Upper" exhibition, curated by Amos Klausner, the Pasadena Museum of California Art asked twenty-six designers to re-imagine one letter from the alphabet, using the illegibility and deconstructive nature of graffiti as their starting point. Design is Play's lowercase letter "a" is derived from Albrecht Dürer's schema for blackletter construction, which was published in 1538. Dürer's line drawing breaks down the letter into different components to reveal its design. Here, the designers subverted this intent by reversing the diagram, flipping the negative spaces to positive ones. The resulting segments were then printed in a palette of modulated colors that further fragment (and deconstruct) the constructed letter. **DESIGN FIRM:** Design is Play **DESIGNERS:** Angie Wang, Mark Fox **CLIENT AND PUBLISHER:** Design is Play **PRIMARY FONTS:** Blackletter, lowercase "a" drawn by Albrecht Dürer

BEING IRVING HARPER • This cover story in *Metropolis* magazine profiles Irving Harper, a designer for George Nelson Associates who created several icons of modern design, including the Marshmallow sofa and the Herman Miller logo. Harper also designed Herman Miller's advertisements. **DESIGN FIRM:** *Metropolis* magazine **ART DIRECTOR:** Criswell Lappin **PHOTOGRAPHER:** James Westman **PUBLISHER:** Bellerophon Publishers **PRIMARY FONT:** Helvetica Compressed

217

THE GREAT POLITICAL THEORIES • *The Great Political Theories* presents key political philosophy writings, from the Greeks to the present, in two volumes. For the theme of each cover, designer Gregg Kulick decided to focus on two central political systems of the 21st century: democracy and communism. Volume two (opposite) "was my visual interpretation of democracy," says Kulick. "I chose the color green to represent the organic nature of the system, and a circle because it is an all-inclusive geometric form. If I had really wanted to capture modern democracy, I could perhaps have included some corporate logos." **ART DIRECTOR:** Robin Bilardello **DESIGNER:** Gregg Kulick **PUBLISHER:** Harper Perennial **PRIMARY FONT:** Helvetica

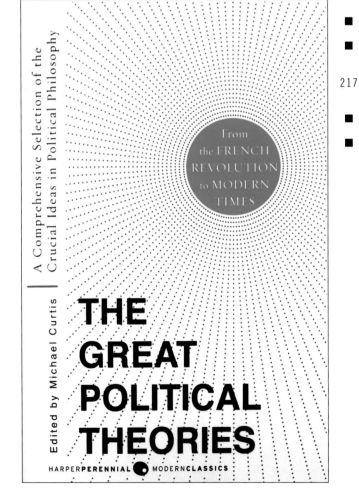

GEOMETRIC

THE SWEET SCIENCE OF SWIMSUITS • The basis for this typographically symbolic composition was molecular chemistry. The letters follow the form of chemical notations. **DESIGN DIRECTOR:** Fred Woodward **DESIGNER:** Anton Loukhnovets **PHOTOGRAPHER:** Richard Burbridge **CLIENT:** *GQ* **PUBLISHER:** Condé Nast **PRIMARY FONT:** Helvetica

VIVA LA RÉVOLUTION WORKSHOP • This workshop poster references "Müller-Brockmann's great Musica Viva posters, while simultaneously alluding to the letterpress printing process through the gear imagery and wood texture," says David Wolske. **ART DIRECTOR, DESIGNER, AND ILLUSTRATOR:** David Wolske **CLIENT:** The J. Willard Marriott Library, University of Utah (Book Arts Program, Special Collections) **PRIMARY FONTS:** Knockout, Trade Gothic

"5E" CINQUIÈME SALLE, PLACE DES ARTS • These poster designs play with the deconstruction of the graphics and the layout, using black and one strong vibrant color. **DESIGN FIRM:** Departement **ART DIRECTOR AND DESIGNER:** Philippe Archontakis **PHOTOGRAPHER:** Thibaut Duverneix **CLIENT:** Place des Arts **PRIMARY FONTS:** Clarendon, Avenir

RING ROAD • This 12" vinyl singles sleeve is the spitting image of Russian Constructivism (Kazimir Malevich in particular). **DESIGN FIRM:** Tomato **ART DIRECTOR AND DESIGNER:** John Warwicker **CLIENT:** Underworld **PRIMARY FONT:** Fournier

GEOMETRIC

KUNSTMARKT 1994. ARTISTS OF CENTRAL SWITZERLAND, STANS • From a distance the type reads perfectly, but up close it is a truly abstract geometric design. **DESIGN FIRM:** Melchior Imboden, Graphic Atelier **ART DIRECTOR AND DESIGNER:** Melchior Imboden **CLIENT:** Gallery Chäslager, Stans **PRINTER:** Bösch Siebdruck AG, Stans **PRIMARY FONT:** Custom

APOLLO • Corporate design for interactive studio Apollo Media, including letterheads, business cards, stickers, and website. **DESIGN FIRM:** Studio Laucke Siebein **ART DIRECTORS:** Dirk Laucke, Johanna Siebein **DESIGNER:** Dirk Laucke **CLIENT:** Apollo Media, Amsterdam **PRIMARY FONT:** Arial

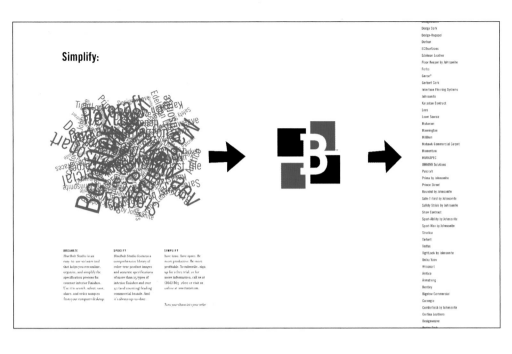

Simplify:

ORGANIZE BlueBolt Studio is an easy- to- use tool bar that helps you streamline, organize, and simplify the specification process for contract interior finishes. Use it to search, select, save, share, and order samples from your computer desktop.

SPECIFY BlueBolt Studio features a comprehensive library of color- true product images and accurate specifications of more than 25 types of interior finishes and over 50 (and counting) leading commercial brands. And it's always up-to-date.

SIMPLIFY Save time. Save space. Be more productive. Be more profitable. To subscribe, sign up for a free trial, or for more information, call us at (866) 865- 2600 or visit us online at www.bmet.com.

Turn your chaos into your order.

BLUEBOLT • Alexander Isley created an identity and communication design for a new suite of software and online tools developed by BlueBolt Networks for the architectural and interior design markets. This loosely composed, somewhat expressionist design uses simple geometry to illuminate the idea of "simplifying" through the typographic equation. **DESIGN FIRM:** Alexander Isley, Inc. **ART DIRECTOR:** Alexander Isley **DESIGNER:** Liesl Kaplan **CLIENT:** BlueBolt Networks, Durham **PRIMARY FONT:** Trade Gothic

221

INSTABLE • Instable is a community of new, talented photographers who recently graduated from Vevey's art school (the CEPV ESAA), in Switzerland. For their first public exhibition, the brief was to put together twelve different artists with their own styles and personalities. To create the exhibition poster, Demian Conrad was inspired by microbacteria and designed several patterns that interact with one another and evoke the idea of biodiversity. The posters are modular and easy to combine into bigger canvases. **DESIGN FIRM:** Demian Conrad Design **ART DIRECTOR AND DESIGNER:** Demian Conrad **CLIENT:** Collectif Instable **PRIMARY FONT:** Akzidenz-Grotesk

GEOMETRIC

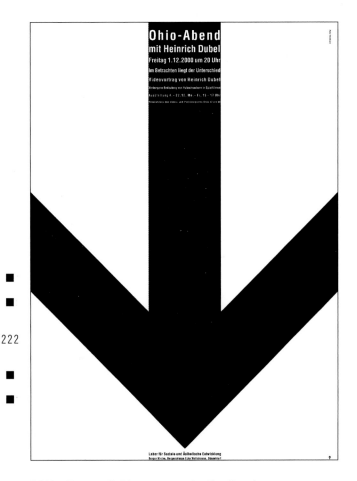

OHIO • Thorsten Nolting, pastor at the City Church in Düsseldorf, instigated a season of events in Berger Church: concerts by DJs (under the subheading "Christian Pop"), an exhibition to which visitors brought their own exhibits, a twenty-four-hour "social experiment," film evenings, clothing collections, an Internet exhibition, open discussions and video speeches, and communal meals with artists, the homeless, and members of the public. To advertise these events, design firm Fons Hickmann m23 was invited to create posters. The design element that holds this poster series together is clarity: the use of black and white, the impact of Helvetica, the minimalism, and the conceptual rigor.
DESIGN FIRM: Fons Hickmann m23 **ART DIRECTOR AND DESIGNER:** Fons Hickmann **CLIENT:** Laboratory for Social and Aesthetic Development **PRIMARY FONT:** Helvetica

137 • This distinctive geometric re-creation of the British flag is an interesting way of illustrating a headline. **DESIGNER:** Ken DeLago **CLIENT:** *Golf Digest* **PUBLISHER:** Condé Nast **PRIMARY FONT:** Helvetica

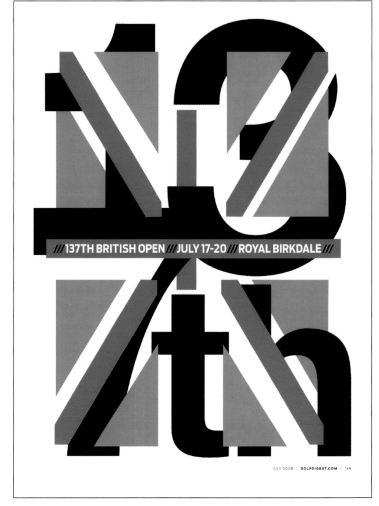

SNS REAAL FONDS • This annual report for the SNS Reaal Fonds (Dutch bank SNS's foundation, which sponsors all kinds of projects in art and culture) has a linen cover that holds together separate dossiers about the organization's structure, statistics, sponsored projects, interviews, and many geometric charts. **DESIGN FIRM:** Studio Laucke Siebein **ART DIRECTORS:** Dirk Laucke, Johanna Siebein **DESIGNER:** Dirk Laucke **CLIENT:** SNS Reaal Fonds, Utrecht **PRIMARY FONTS:** Futura, Quadraat

G8 SUMMIT, HOKKAIDO • This logo for the G8 summit is a variation on circles, all intertwined to create a geometric "8." **DESIGN FIRM:** Tomato **ART DIRECTOR AND DESIGNER:** John Warwicker **CLIENT AND PUBLISHER:** Government of Sapporo, Japan **PRIMARY FONT:** Custom

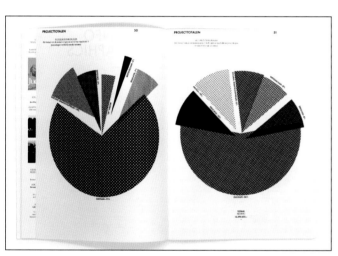

223

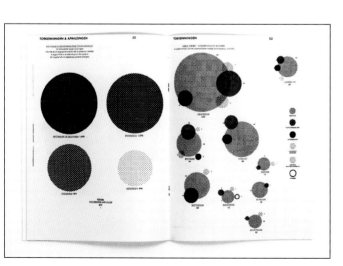

GEOMETRIC

TIHANY DESIGN IDENTITY • Adam Tihany is one of the most celebrated interior architects of today. His logo and identity are based on a grid sheet to evoke architectural drawings. The letters "t" and "d" are associated with blueprints and chairs. The identity is Bauhaus-inspired, very geometric and minimalist. **DESIGN FIRM:** Mirko Ilić Corp. **ART DIRECTOR AND DESIGNER:** Mirko Ilić **CLIENT:** Tihany Design **PRIMARY FONT:** Custom

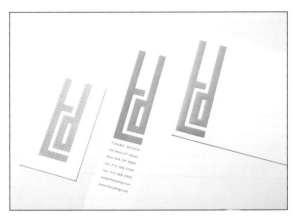

SHAKESPEARE IN THE PARK • The poster campaign for the 2005 Shakespeare in the Park productions of *As You Like It* and *The Two Gentlemen of Verona* was inspired by street typography and the traditions of theatrical promotion – as was the identity created by Paula Scher for The Public Theater. **DESIGN FIRM:** Pentagram **ART DIRECTOR:** Paula Scher **DESIGNERS:** Paula Scher, Julia Hoffmann **CLIENT:** The Public Theater **PRIMARY FONT:** Akzidenz-Grotesk

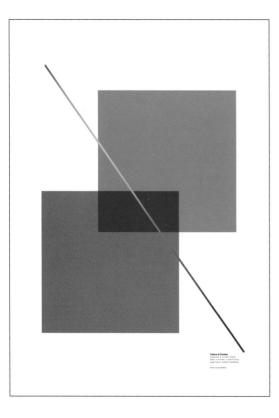

COLORS & FORMS • This series of posters represents "a graphic designer's insight into basic colors." **DESIGN FIRM:** GVA Studio **CLIENT:** Self **PRIMARY FONT:** Custom

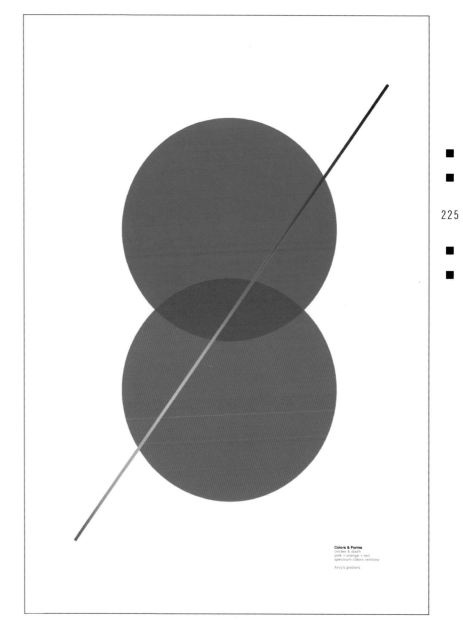

GEOMETRIC

BRASILIA 50 POSTER • Fifty designers were asked to pay homage to the city of Brasilia and the legacy of Brazilian architect Oscar Niemeyer. The designers were inspired by his sumptuous and organic architecture, and by one of his quotes: "It is not the right angle that attracts me, nor the straight line, hard and inflexible, created by man. What attracts me is the free and sensual curve – the curve that I find in the mountains of my country, in the sinuous course of its rivers, in the body of the beloved woman." **DESIGN FIRM:** Sawdust **ART DIRECTORS AND DESIGNERS:** Jonathan Quainton, Rob Gonzalez **CLIENT:** Brasilia Prima **CLIENT:** Brasilia Prima **PRIMARY FONT:** Custom typography

226

Brasília
50th Anniversary

Design by Sawdust

"It is not the right angle that attracts me, nor the straight line, hard and inflexible, created by man. What attracts me is the free and sensual curve – the curve that I find in the mountains of my country, in the sinuous course of its rivers, in the body of the beloved woman".

— Oscar Niemeyer

EMBAJADA DEL BRASIL

CENTRO METROPOLITANO DE DISEÑO

PLAN
arquitectura | interiorismo

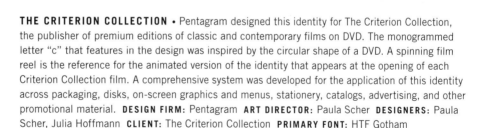

THE CRITERION COLLECTION • Pentagram designed this identity for The Criterion Collection, the publisher of premium editions of classic and contemporary films on DVD. The monogrammed letter "c" that features in the design was inspired by the circular shape of a DVD. A spinning film reel is the reference for the animated version of the identity that appears at the opening of each Criterion Collection film. A comprehensive system was developed for the application of this identity across packaging, disks, on-screen graphics and menus, stationery, catalogs, advertising, and other promotional material. **DESIGN FIRM:** Pentagram **ART DIRECTOR:** Paula Scher **DESIGNERS:** Paula Scher, Julia Hoffmann **CLIENT:** The Criterion Collection **PRIMARY FONT:** HTF Gotham

APOTHEEK KIDS • At the Apotheek Kids activity day, children were invited to approach colors and shapes in a fun way. For this occasion, GVA Studio designed the Apotheek Kids logo, an animals coloring book, posters, and postcards. Watercolors and paint brushes were available on site for the children and their parents. They filled pages and pages of Apotheek animals. **DESIGN FIRM:** GVA Studio **CLIENT:** Self **PRIMARY FONT:** Custom

GEOMETRIC

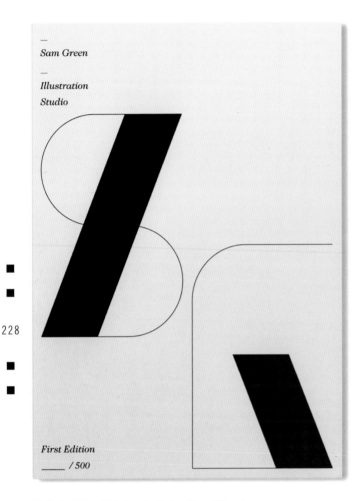

SAM GREEN • This is a limited-edition A3 mailer with "S" and "G" letters made from radically thick and thin geometric shapes **DESIGN FIRM:** Sawdust **ART DIRECTORS AND DESIGNERS:** Jonathan Quainton, Rob Gonzalez **ILLUSTRATOR:** Sam Green **CLIENT:** Sam Green **PRIMARY FONT:** Custom

GROUP8 • Based on the proportions of the infinity symbol, GVA Studio developed a grid that increases to infinity, so that "∞" (or "8") becomes the essential constructive element on this promotional mailing card. **DESIGN FIRM:** GVA Studio **CLIENT:** group8 **PRIMARY FONT:** Custom

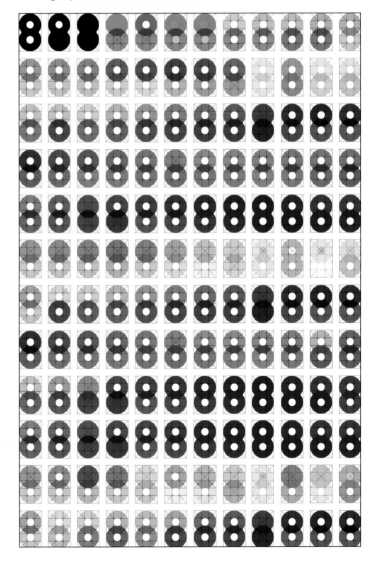

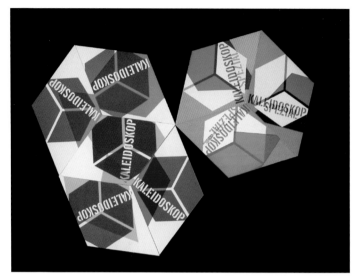

KALEIDOSKOP FLYERS • The kaleidoscope, with its random geometry, is the basis for these flyers advertising concerts and parties at Berlin's famous Cafe Moskau. **DESIGN FIRM:** Jacques Magiera (materia.li) **ART DIRECTOR AND DESIGNER:** Jacques Magiera **CLIENT:** Best Works **PRIMARY FONT:** Trade Gothic

IGNORANCE • This editorial illustration for *Wired* magazine is reminiscent of the colors and forms in Ladislav Sutnar's work. **DESIGN FIRM:** Oliver Munday Group (OMG) **ART DIRECTOR:** Christy Shepard **DESIGNER:** Oliver Munday **CLIENT:** *Wired* magazine **PUBLISHER:** Condé Nast **PRIMARY FONT:** Bodoni

GEOMETRIC

ALL YOU NEED IS LOVE • The repetition of the word "love" adds a vibration and brings tension to this otherwise clichéd phrase. **DESIGN FIRM:** Leslie Moore **CLIENT:** Self **PRIMARY FONT:** Code

BOOKA SHADE – LOVE • For Booka Shade's fourth album and its singles and promotional material the designers used a custom font designed in 2004 to construct the Booka Shade logo. This poster was a promotional piece set in the Booka Shade font showing the word "love." **DESIGN FIRM:** Hort **ART DIRECTOR AND DESIGNER:** Hort **CLIENT:** Get Physical Music **PRIMARY FONT:** Selfmade

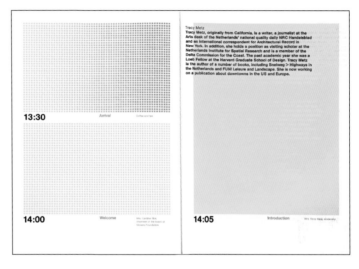

SIKKENS PRIZE • This booklet was designed on the occasion of the awarding ceremony of the Sikkens Prize to Art Angel and Krijn de Koning. **DESIGN FIRM:** Studio Laucke Siebein **ART DIRECTORS:** Dirk Laucke, Johanna Siebein **DESIGNERS:** Dirk Laucke, Marc Karpstein **CLIENT:** AkzoNobel Decorative Coatings/Sikkens Foundation, Sassenheim, NL **PRIMARY FONT:** Helvetica

ANGEL-A • Art deco was the inspiration for this logotype for music artist Angel-A. **DESIGN FIRM:** Sawdust **ART DIRECTORS AND DESIGNERS:** Jonathan Quainton, Rob Gonzalez **CLIENT:** Angel-A **PRIMARY FONT:** Custom

GEOMETRIC

THE BEST CREATIVE NONFICTION, VOL. 2 • What can be more purely geometric than circles? This otherwise typographically minimal design relies on colored circles to add tension and allure.
DESIGN FIRM: Rodrigo Corral Design
ART DIRECTOR: Ingsu Liu **DESIGNERS:** Rodrigo Corral, Mark Melnick
PUBLISHER: W.W. Norton **PRIMARY FONT:** HTF Mercury Semibold

232

THE BEST CREATIVE
NONFICTION

VOL. 2

EDITED BY

LEE GUTKIND

MVSICA • This limited-edition CD packaging featured removable gold latex panels covering all text, including the tracklist and the front title. Each CD came with a random-coloured plastic counter with which to scratch off the gold latex (or not). The typography underneath these gold panels is "aesthetically minimal throughout," says designer Rob Gonzales, "because it's a down tempo compilation by purists within the techno genre, so the packaging was designed to reflect that." **DESIGN FIRM:** Sawdust **ART DIRECTORS AND DESIGNERS:** Jonathan Quainton, Rob Gonzalez **CLIENT:** Fine Art Recordings **PRIMARY FONT:** Custom

DREW BARRYMORE • The domino conceit that serves as both headline and illustration also represents Drew Barrymore's initials. **DESIGN FIRM:** *W* magazine **ART DIRECTOR AND DESIGNER:** Nathalie Kirsheh **PHOTOGRAPHERS:** Mert Alas, Marcus Piggott **PUBLISHER:** Condé Nast **PRIMARY FONT:** Custom

GEOMETRIC

174 Duane Street between Hudson and Greenwich Streets (across from Duane Park)

234

MONDO CANE • Terry Koppel claims that this poster has the Paul Rand fingerprint, but it is ever so slight. Instead, this design echoes the composition of a printing sample. **DESIGN FIRM:** T. Koppel Design **ART DIRECTOR AND DESIGNER:** Terry Koppel **PHOTOGRAPHER:** Patrick Parrish **CLIENT:** Mondo Cane **PUBLISHER:** Mondo Cane **PRIMARY FONTS:** Grotesque Bold, Bodoni Italic

JAZZ AT LINCOLN CENTER • In order to celebrate the relevance of jazz and to communicate the true experience of live music, designer Bobby C. Martin Jr. had to tap into the emotional benefits of attending a Jazz at Lincoln Center concert. "We worked with the musicians to better understand the soul of the music, then developed a graphic approach that visualized the unique experience of contemporary jazz," Martin explains. **DESIGN FIRM:** Jazz at Lincoln Center **ART DIRECTOR AND DESIGNER:** Bobby C. Martin Jr. **PHOTOGRAPHER:** Frank Stewart **CLIENT:** Jazz at Lincoln Center **PRIMARY FONT:** Gotham

GEORGE ORWELL SERIES • The design of these book covers for a series of books by George Orwell was influenced by vintage science textbooks and, says Jamie Keenan, "getting so close to television screens that the picture stops meaning anything." **DESIGN FIRM:** Keenan **ART DIRECTOR:** Jim Stoddart **DESIGNER:** Jamie Keenan **CLIENT:** Penguin UK **PRIMARY FONT:** Univers

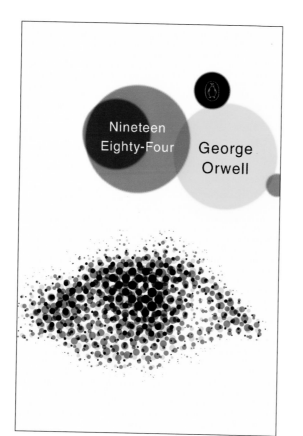

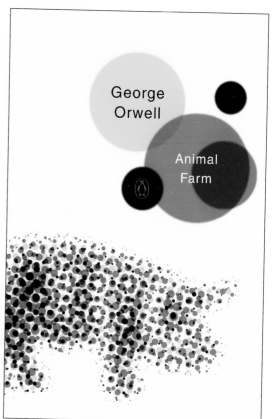

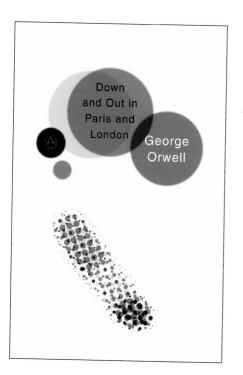

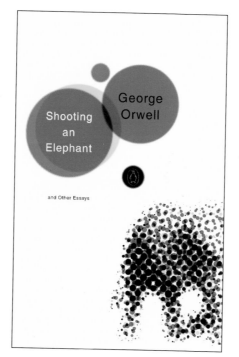

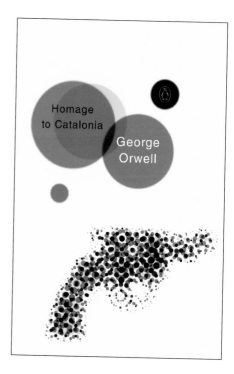

GEOMETRIC

■
■

236

■
■

Movie Poster for *Blow Up*: A Film by Michaelangelo Antonioni

BLOW UP • This movie poster, which has a taste of Saul Bass, was "inspired by vintage Italian ski posters," says Lisa Maione. **DESIGN FIRM:** Lisa Maione **DESIGNER:** Lisa Maione **CLIENT:** Richard Rose (Faculty Advisor) **PRIMARY FONT:** DIN

BLOW UP

A FILM BY
MICHAELANGELO ANTONIONI

BOOKA SHADE TOUR • Using one of their custom fonts to construct the Booka Shade logo and "set every information just straight, with some little details regarding title or product," design firm Hort created these two posters: one tour poster and another announcing the release date of the album "More." **DESIGN FIRM:** Hort **ART DIRECTOR AND DESIGNER:** Hort **CLIENT:** Get Physical Music **PRIMARY FONTS:** Custom, Akzidenz-Grotesk

DJ SOLO • Commissioned by a DJ to design a logotype for use on merchandise and apparel, design firm Faith created an image that is entirely rooted in geometric purity and decoration. **DESIGN FIRM:** Faith **ART DIRECTOR AND DESIGNER:** Paul Sych **CLIENT:** DJ Solo **PRIMARY FONT:** Custom

GEOMETRIC

N
A
O
M
I

WATTS IS IN YOUR PANTS

photographs by **&** *MARK SELIGER*

spectators smolder

Say g'day to the Australian ingenue who makes sock garters, suspenders &

Tuxedo pants and shirt by Helmut Lang. Suspenders by Trafalgar. Bra by Cosabella. Diamond earrings by Erica Courtney, necklace by Loree Rodkin and ring by Neil Lane.

238

NAOMI • Constructivist aesthetics inform this editorial title page, with asymmetrical and geometric shapes running rampant through the composition. **DESIGN FIRM:** *GQ* **DESIGN DIRECTOR:** Fred Woodward **DESIGNER:** Ken DeLago **CLIENT:** Condé Nast **PRIMARY FONT:** Gotham

16.01 SPLASH PAGE • A panoply of geometric and random shapes creates a dramatic collage effect. **DESIGN FIRM:** *Wired* magazine **CREATIVE DIRECTOR:** Scott Dadich **DESIGNERS:** Maili Holiman, Scott Dadich **ILLUSTRATOR:** 2x4 NY **PUBLISHER:** Condé Nast **PRIMARY FONT:** Custom

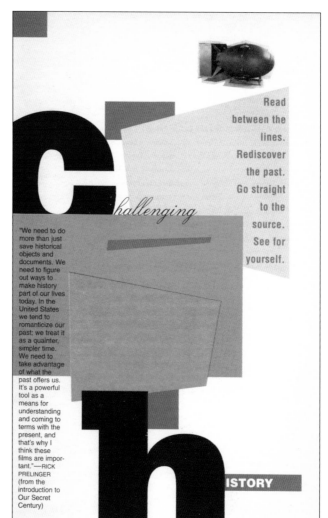

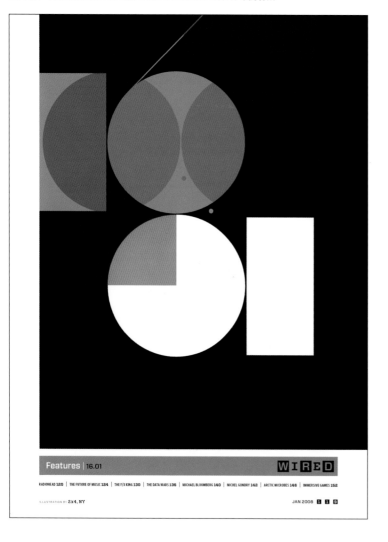

CHALLENGING HISTORY • Based on bad 1950s collage design, this very low-budget two-color design work was created using public domain art. It was commissioned by Voyager for an interactive CD. **DESIGN FIRM:** T. Koppel Design **ART DIRECTOR AND DESIGNER:** Terry Koppel **ILLUSTRATOR AND PHOTOGRAPHER:** Found art (public domain) **PUBLISHER:** Voyager **PRIMARY FONTS:** Alternate Gothic, Helvetica Neue Bold, Giza

GEOMETRIC

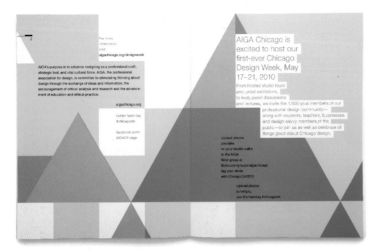

STUDIO WALKS (AIGA CHICAGO) • The AIGA's *Studio Walks* book is a small pocket guide showcasing the graphic design studios and firms that participated in Chicago's 2010 Design Week. In addition to studio and firm profiles, it features maps of guided tours and routes for walking from one studio to the next, and then to the afterparty. The visual theme for the 2010 Design Week was based on three geometric shapes: the circle, the square, and the triangle. Here, these simple forms were used to create a new "landscape" for the event. **DESIGN FIRM:** Plural **ART DIRECTORS AND DESIGNERS:** Jeremiah Chiu, Renata Graw **ILLUSTRATOR:** Plural **PHOTOGRAPHER:** Various **CLIENT AND PUBLISHER:** AIGA Chicago **PRIMARY FONTS:** Helvetica, Custom Type

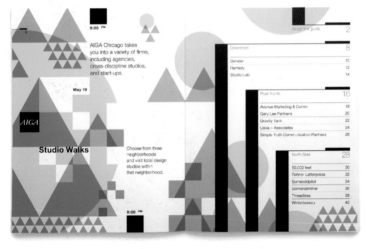

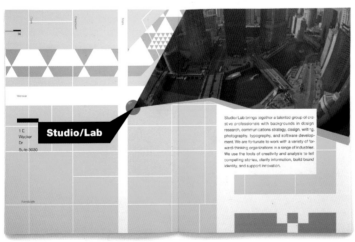

SIXTY SIXTY SIXTY • This display typeface was created during a workshop held at RISD in 2005. The challenge was to use two modules to create the entire set of letters. **DESIGN FIRM:** Underware **DESIGNERS:** Lisa Maione, Asad Pervaiz **PRIMARY FONT:** Custom

HOPOS • In this lively series of covers for *Hopos* (the journal of the International Society for the History of Philosophy of Science) bright colors and geometric shapes echo the quieter typography. **DESIGN FIRM:** Salamander Hill Design **DESIGNER:** David Drummond **CLIENT:** Ashley Towne **PUBLISHER:** University of Chicago Press **PRIMARY FONTS:** Helvetica, Futura, Garamond

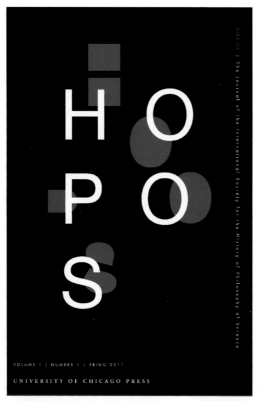

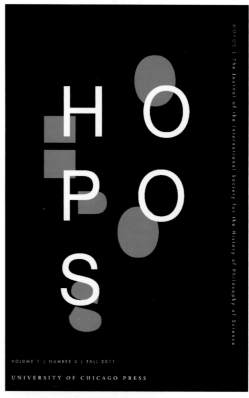

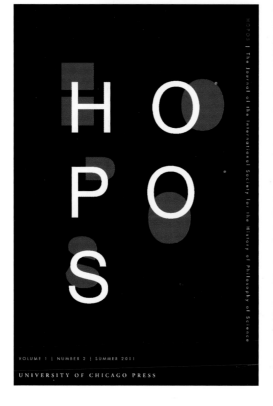

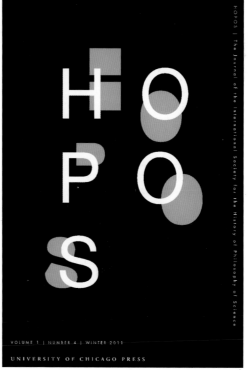

241

OPTICAL

Op (or optical) Art was a late modern aesthetic. But even the very orthodox Swiss school attempted to create more dimensions on two-dimensional surfaces. This section includes classic approaches and avant-garde modernisms twisted and turned to add illusionary weight to the printed page (and now to the LED screen).

ECDC – DANSOMÈTRE • Dansomètre, or Espace de Création pour la Danse Contemporaine (ECDC), is a space dedicated to the development of small Swiss dance companies. It is based in the city of Vevey, in Switzerland. The visual concept for this poster is inspired by the work of Étienne-Jules Marey, the inventor of the Chronophotographe (an instrument that could take twelve consecutive frames a second). In fact, Vevey is also the Swiss capital of photography so the technique used in this poster is a fitting tribute to movement, dance, and photography. **DESIGN FIRM:** Demian Conrad Design **ART DIRECTOR, DESIGNER, AND PHOTOGRAPHER:** Demian Conrad **CLIENT:** Ville de Vevey (Service Culturel), Switzerland **PRIMARY FONT:** Akzidenz-Grotesk

PHYSICS • Andrei Robu was commissioned to create a poster for this classic Penguin book. He used one of his favorite symbols as his reference: the eye of providence. **DESIGN FIRM:** Andrei Robu. com **ART DIRECTOR, DESIGNER, AND ILLUSTRATOR:** Andrei Robu **CLIENT:** Type Goods **PRIMARY FONT:** Helvetica Neue

DESIGN IS PLAY • "Our site design," says Mark Fox, "is based on the idea of different rooms: the studio (where we present our professional work) and the beautiful room (where we credit our sources, collaborators, and inspirations). We sought to translate our print sensibilities to this non-print medium through the use of a flexible grid, clear typography, and dynamic negative space." **DESIGN FIRM:** Design is Play **ART DIRECTOR:** Angie Wang **DESIGNERS:** Angie Wang, Mark Fox **PHOTOGRAPHER:** Annie Chen **CLIENT AND PUBLISHER:** Design is Play **PRIMARY FONTS:** Helvetica Neue Bold, Lucida Grande

OPTICAL

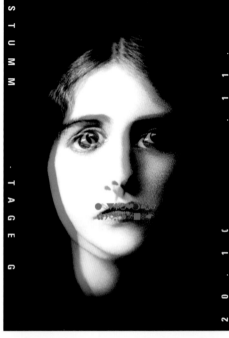

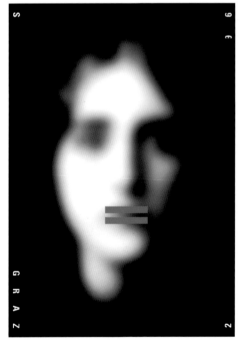

WHEN EYES COULD STILL SPEAK • With suggestions of early 20th-century Russian and German avant-garde photography, this series of four posters addresses the idea of silence, film, and vision. **DESIGN FIRM:** Fons Hickmann m23 **ART DIRECTOR AND DESIGNER:** Fons Hickmann **PHOTOGRAPHER:** Henny Porten **CLIENT:** Silent Movie Festival **PRIMARY FONT:** Univers

FANATICISM

ON THE USES OF AN IDEA

ALBERTO TOSCANO

FANATICISM • Fanaticism is usually seen as a deviant or extreme variant of an already irrational set of religious beliefs but Alberto Toscano's counter-history explores the critical role fanaticism played in forming modern politics and the liberal state. The type tries to express obsession, intensity, even aggression, and gradually transforms into the title. "I was interested in the positive/negative spaces formed by the letters, revealing sections of the word," says Gary Tooth. "I wanted the final result to be both beautiful and slightly disturbing." **DESIGN FIRM:** Empire Design Studio **ART DIRECTOR, DESIGNER, AND ILLUSTRATOR:** Gary Tooth **CLIENT:** Bob Bharma **PUBLISHER:** Verso Books **PRIMARY FONT:** DIN

245

OPTICAL

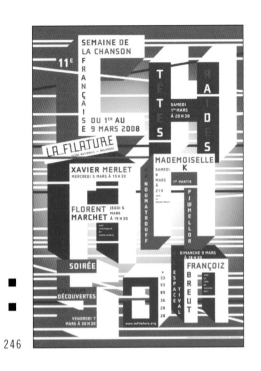

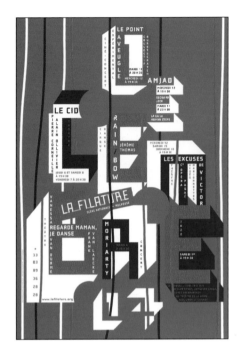

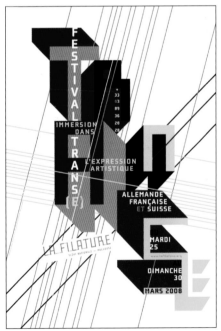

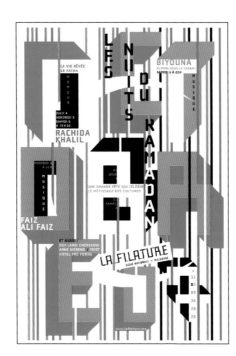

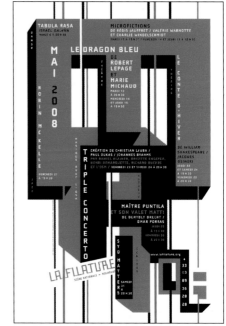

FILATURE • Arts center La Filature (French for "spinning mill") is based in Mulhouse, in the triangle where France, Switzerland, and Germany "meet." For these monthly season posters, the designers' idea was to create interwoven graphics to reflect the multiple art forms (film, music, dance, theater, and others) that cross paths at La Filature. **ART DIRECTORS AND DESIGNERS:** Anette Lenz, Vincent Perrottet **CLIENT:** La Filature, Scène Nationale de Mulhouse **PRIMARY FONTS:** Helvetica Rounded, Stencil Gothic

OPTICAL

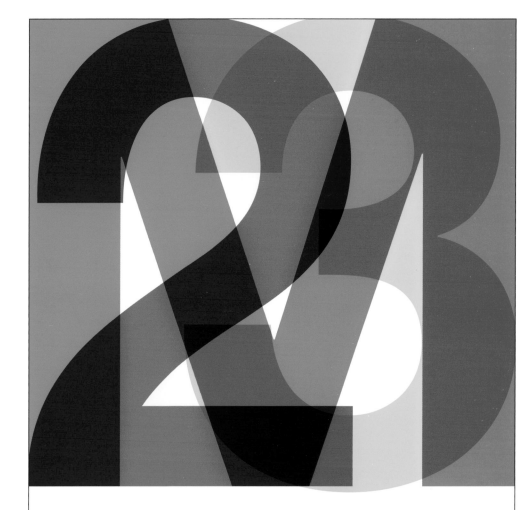

Fons Hickmann m23
razstava grafičnega oblikovanja

NLB Galerija Avla
Trg republike 2 / Ljubljana / Slovenija

20.11.2008 - 22.01.2009
pripravil Emzin

M23 POSTER • In this poster for his solo exhibition in Ljubljana, Fons Hickmann uses overlays and transparencies to trigger an interesting optical sensation. **DESIGN FIRM:** Fons Hickmann m23 **ART DIRECTOR AND DESIGNER:** Fons Hickmann **CLIENT:** Emzin, Slovenia **PRIMARY FONT:** Helvetica

LOOSE COLLECTIVE • This logo, created for design firm Loose Collective, "reflects the idea of different elements coming together to form a whole," says Graham Jones. "The type is more neutral, so that it doesn't visually lean toward one style. Modernist grid structures are also implemented for maximum legibility and clarity." **DESIGN FIRM:** Loose Collective **ART DIRECTOR AND DESIGNER:** Graham Jones **CLIENT:** Loose Collective **PRIMARY FONT:** Avant Garde Gothic

TARSILA DO AMARAL • The major influences behind the design of this catalog for an exhibition about Brazilian modernist painter Tarsila do Amaral are Dada, concrete poetry, and modernism. The large "S" is used to create an illusion of transparency. **ART DIRECTOR:** Guillermo Nagore **DESIGNER:** Kim Bost **CLIENT AND PUBLISHER:** Fundación Juan March **PRIMARY FONTS:** Found type specimen, Venus Extrabold Condensed

OPTICAL

CIRCLING THE DRAIN • In this book of short stories about women going slightly crazy, designer Archie Ferguson explains that he "tried to wed the tone of the cover design with that of the book's title." The twirling type and image imply that something is out of whack. **DESIGN FIRM:** Archie Ferguson Design **ART DIRECTOR AND DESIGNER:** Archie Ferguson **PHOTOGRAPHER:** Cody **CLIENT AND PUBLISHER:** Weisbach Books **PRIMARY FONT:** Futura

MMKK LOGOTYPE • This logotype, created for the Museum of Modern Art of Kärnten (MMKK) in Austria, gives the impression of receding into space. **DESIGN FIRM:** Fons Hickmann m23 **ART DIRECTOR:** Fons Hickmann **DESIGNERS:** Fons Hickmann, Christof Nardin, Christina Graeni **CLIENT:** Museum of Modern Art, Kärnten, Austria **PRIMARY FONT:** Custom

FLIFEST • This poster for a multidisciplinary arts event, with many projections, was a good opportunity for Gramlich to multiply pure colors to generate new forms and colors. The direct influences are Russian Constructivism, Swiss typography, and, he says, "as always, a search for new forms of expression." **DESIGN FIRM:** gggrafik **ART DIRECTOR, DESIGNER, AND ILLUSTRATOR:** Götz Gramlich **CLIENT:** Flifest, Barcelona **PRIMARY FONTS:** Gotham, Le Typographe (by Julien Priez)

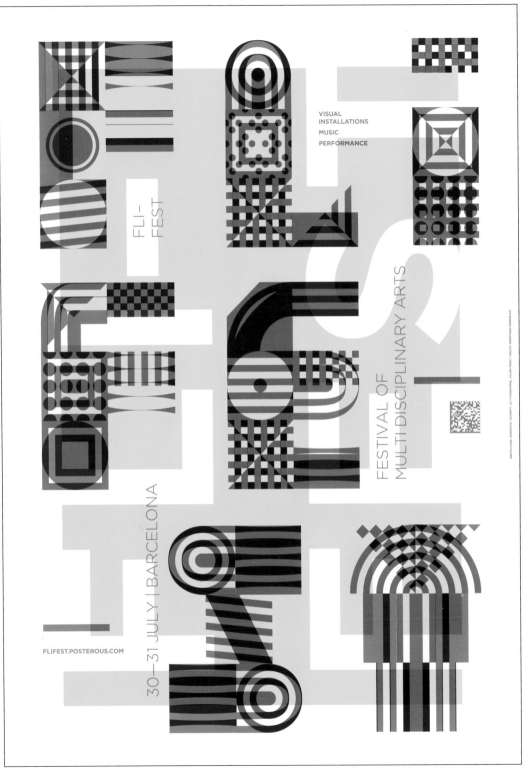

251

OPTICAL

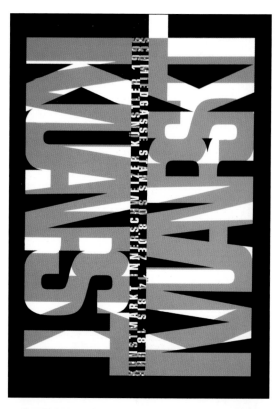

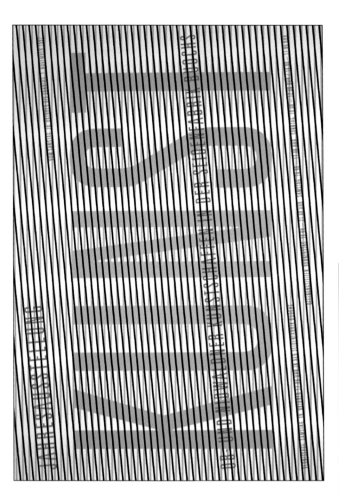

**KUNSTMARKT: ARTISTS OF CENTRAL
SWITZERLAND, STANS •** These posters use a
modern aesthetic that mixes Russian Constructivism
with dynamic optical conceits (the common target,
overprints, and transparencies, for instance).
DESIGN FIRM: Melchior Imboden, Graphic Atelier
ART DIRECTOR AND DESIGNER: Melchior Imboden
CLIENT: Gallery Chäslager, Stans **PRIMARY FONT:**
Univers Condensed

OPTICAL

WEDER ENTWEDER NOCH ODER • The deliberate confusion in the title ("Neither, either, nor, or") is reflected in the shifted logic of the typography. **DESIGN FIRM:** L2M3 Kommunikationsdesign GmbH **ART DIRECTOR:** Sascha Lobel **DESIGNERS:** Ina Bauer, Sascha Lobe **CLIENT:** Württembergischer Kunstverein Stuttgart **PRIMARY FONTS:** Monotype Grotesque, Avant Garde

LATE SPOT • This poster was created for the Late Spot club at the Willisau Jazz Festival. The club opens after the festival's regular jazz concerts end. Götz Gramlich made a font out of forms that Niklaus Troxler had used in his designs for the festival, and he overprinted the type with a nightglowing color that could only be seen at night, when the Late Spot is opened. **DESIGN FIRM:** gggrafik **ART DIRECTOR, DESIGNER, AND ILLUSTRATOR:** Götz Gramlich **CLIENT:** Flifest, Barcelona **PRIMARY FONT:** Custom

20 YEARS AFTER THE FALL OF THE BERLIN WALL • This poster for a concert celebrating Berlin's freedom employs a yin-and-yang typographic conceit that suggests the East, the West, and the wall that separated them. **DESIGN FIRM:** Fons Hickmann m23 **DESIGNER:** Thomas Schrott **CLIENT:** ROC Berlin **PRIMARY FONT:** Helvetica

TILLY DEVINE • Tilly Devine is a McLaren Vale Shiraz named after the notorious Sydney madam and bootlegger of the 1920s. Tilly Devine's bootlegging operation was so successful that her name was adopted as rhyming slang for "wine." The design here evokes the fact that, in her heyday, Tilly could be found either in cocktail bars or behind prison bars. **DESIGN FIRM:** Parallax Design **DESIGNER:** Kellie Campbell-Illingworth **CLIENT:** Antipodean Vintners **PRIMARY FONTS:** Handlettered, Franklin Gothic, Newzald

OPTICAL

INVITATION CARDS FOR SCHEIBLER MITTE • This is a series of invitations created for Berlin-based contemporary art gallery Scheibler Mitte. The diagonal stripes are reminiscent of the red signal lines at the entrance of the former industrial area in which the gallery is located. **DESIGN FIRM:** Studio Laucke Siebein **ART DIRECTOR:** Dirk Laucke, Johanna Siebein **DESIGNER:** Dirk Laucke **CLIENT:** Scheibler Mitte, Berlin **PRIMARY FONT:** Akzidenz-Grotesk

256

Anthony Goicolea

ScheiblerMitte
1. Mai–3. Juli 2010
Eröffnung
30. April 18–21 Uhr

ScheiblerMitte
6. Februar–1. April 2010
Eröffnung
5. Februar, 18–21 Uhr

Thomas Rentmeister
Der Staatsanwalt

METAPHORICAL

Turning type into double entendres (or more) began in the 19th century, if not before, but was continued in a streamlined, sophisticated manner in the 20th century. Metaphorical type – or type as picture – continues to be a key component of the visual pun and a popular means of communicating more than one message at once.

WOW • Andrei Robu has one definitive answer when talking about the influence for the logo: "The EYE of PROVIDENCE." What else is left to be said? **DESIGN FIRM:** Andrei Robu. com **ART DIRECTOR, DESIGNER, AND ILLUSTRATOR:** Andrei Robu **CLIENT:** Type Goods **PRIMARY FONT:** Custom

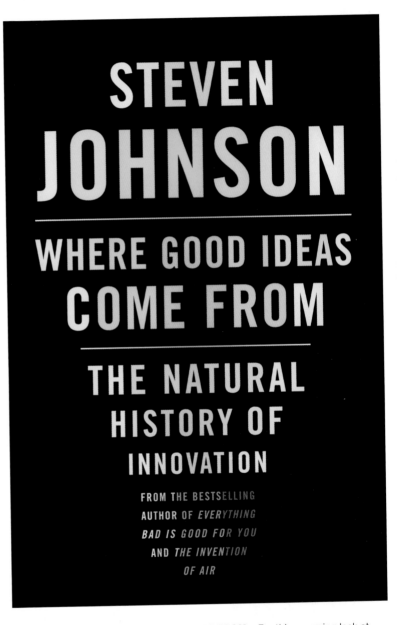

WHERE GOOD IDEAS COME FROM • For this sweeping look at innovation, which spans nearly the whole of human history, the designer notes: "I've always liked anything that can be two things simultaneously." Hence the typography as light bulb. **DESIGN FIRM:** Keenan **ART DIRECTOR:** Helen Yentus **DESIGNER:** Jamie Keenan **CLIENT:** Riverhead Books **PRIMARY FONT:** Trade Gothic

HOW TO SUCCEED IN BUSINESS WITHOUT REALLY TRYING

MUSIC AND LYRICS BY FRANK LOESSER
BOOK BY ABE BURROWS, JACK WEINSTOCK & WILLIE GILBER
DIRECTED BY DANIEL GOLDSTEIN
CHOREOGRAPHY BY BYRON EASLEY, MUSIC DIRECTION BY THOMAS DOUGLAS

NOV 12 THRU 21

www.drama.cmu.edu

Carnegie Mellon
DRAMA

THE GRAPES OF WRATH

FRANK GALATI ADAPTED FROM JOHN STEINBECK'S NOVEL
DIRECTED BY BARBARA MACKENZIE-WOOD

OCT 1 THRU 10

www.drama.cmu.edu

Carnegie Mellon
DRAMA

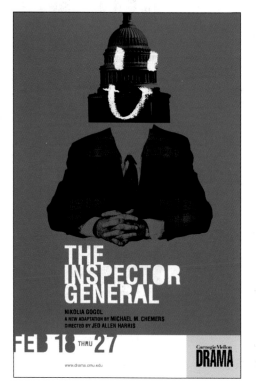

THE INSPECTOR GENERAL

NIKOLIA GOGOL
A NEW ADAPTATION BY MICHAEL M. CHEMERS
DIRECTED BY JED ALLEN HARRIS

FEB 18 THRU 27

www.drama.cmu.edu

Carnegie Mellon
DRAMA

RICHARD III

WILLIAM SHAKESPEARE
DIRECTED BY MATT GRAY

APR 15 THRU 24

www.drama.cmu.edu

Carnegie Mellon
DRAMA

CARNEGIE MELLON UNIVERSITY SCHOOL OF DRAMA – SEASON POSTERS • The designers say they were not "pursuing a specific influence" beyond introducing a simple graphic approach that might be reminiscent of the modernist poster design of the 1950s and 1960s, "intentionally limiting the number of design 'tricks' and trying to inject some graphic wit while using an economy of elements. The primary font is Helvetica, which fits in nicely with the aesthetic. As the font also happened to be the corporate font of the client, it made sense from a branding perspective. Additionally, filling in the counters and crushing the leading gave the font a bit more personality and made it slightly more interesting. All these combined elements created a nice visual language that could spread across four plays." **DESIGN FIRM:** Wall-to-Wall Studios **ART DIRECTORS:** Larkin Werner, James Nesbitt **DESIGNERS:** Larkin Werner, Doug Dean **CLIENT:** Carnegie Mellon University School of Drama **PRIMARY FONT:** Helvetica

METAPHORICAL

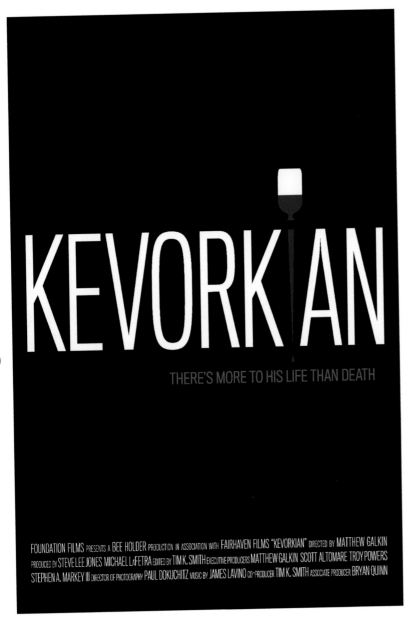

KEVORKIAN

THERE'S MORE TO HIS LIFE THAN DEATH

FOUNDATION FILMS PRESENTS A BEE HOLDER PRODUCTION IN ASSOCIATION WITH FAIRHAVEN FILMS "KEVORKIAN" DIRECTED BY MATTHEW GALKIN PRODUCED BY STEVE LEE JONES MICHAEL LaFETRA EDITED BY TIM K. SMITH EXECUTIVE PRODUCERS MATTHEW GALKIN SCOTT ALTOMARE TROY POWERS STEPHEN A. MARKEY III DIRECTOR OF PHOTOGRAPHY PAUL DOKUCHITZ MUSIC BY JAMES LAVINO CO-PRODUCER TIM K. SMITH ASSOCIATE PRODUCER BRYAN QUINN

THE ACT OF LOVE • This book is about a man who believes that love is about suffering and, as a result, wants his wife to cheat on him. "I thought Cupid's arrow was the perfect symbol for the main character," explains Catherine Casalino. She also wanted to go for a very simple and clean design with this cover. "I have always loved Alvin Lustig's work and I felt that was the right direction for this very complex, idea-driven book." **DESIGN FIRM:** Catherine Casalino Design **ART DIRECTOR:** Jackie Seow **DESIGNER AND ILLUSTRATOR:** Catherine Casalino **CLIENT:** Simon & Schuster **PRIMARY FONTS:** ITC Century, Cloister, Sackers Gothic

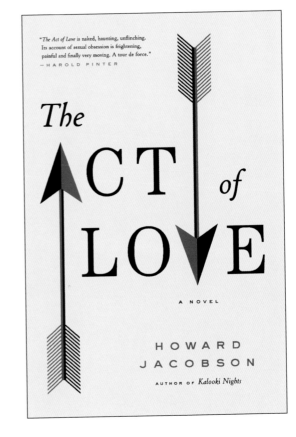

KEVORKIAN • This poster was commissioned to advertise a documentary film about Dr Jack Kevorkian. Using clean typography, the metaphoric – and mnemonic – element is the poisonous drip as the "i": simple and poignant. **DESIGN FIRM:** Little White Bird **ART DIRECTOR AND DESIGNER:** Chloe Weiss Galkin **CLIENTS:** Fairhaven Films, Bee Holder Productions, Foundation Films **PRIMARY FONT:** Titling Gothic

SVA: TO HELP SEE POSSIBILITIES • This was a subway campaign for the School of Visual Arts, New York. "We created an eye-chart that plays a visual trick," says Ilić. "The letters and edges are made out of little objects and have jagged edges. At first it appears almost as if it were out of focus. Only up close can one see the little elements, like little toy soldiers. They are different objects that are related to art." **DESIGN FIRM:** Mirko Ilić Corp. **CREATIVE DIRECTOR:** Anthony Rhodes **ART DIRECTOR:** Michael Walsh **DESIGNER AND ILLUSTRATOR:** Mirko Ilić/Mirko Ilić Corp. **CLIENT:** The School of Visual Arts, New York **PRIMARY FONTS:** Custom, Gotham

261

METAPHORICAL

THE YEAR IN CULTURE: 2009 • For this cover of the Arts & Leisure supplement in *The New York Times*, Muddyum Choudhury conflates crossword puzzles and Piet Mondrian into a crossword boogie-woogie.
DESIGN FIRM: Muddyum **ART DIRECTOR:** Paul Jean **DESIGNER:** Muddyum Choudhury **CLIENT:** *The New York Times* **PRIMARY FONT:** Helvetica Light

Arts&LEISURE

The New York Times

SUNDAY, DECEMBER 20, 2009

ACROSS

1 ___ Architecture Prize (annual Hyatt Foundation award)
6 "When We Was ___" (George Harrison tune)
7 Painting seen in "The Da Vinci Code"
10 French Fauvist painter
13 He performed a Bach cello suite at Senator Edward M. Kennedy's funeral
15 2009 Pixar blockbuster
16 Honorary Oscar recipient in 2009
17 Melvin Purvis portrayer in "Public Enemies"

19 "It's pretty but is it ___?" (Kipling quote)
21 Prime-time drama that ended its 15 year run in 2009
23 Met-based ballet company, for short
24 "___ the Whopper" (Season 21 premiere episode of "The Simpsons")
25 S-shaped architectural molding
27 "Love Is the Answer" singer's 1983 film
29 New York Philharmonic's Cynthia Phelps, for one
30 Winslow Homer genre
31 Slender part of a violin

DOWN

2 Broadway award
3 New N.E.A. head Landesman
4 Mezzo-soprano who received Kennedy Center Honors in 2009
5 Network being bought by Comcast
8 Home of the choreographer Mugur Sundar
9 2 Down winner in 2009 for "Blithe Spirit"
10 2009 film based on a Japanese media franchise
11 Top-rated prime-time series in each of the past five years, for short

12 "Fritz the Cat" creator and Genesis illustrator in 2009
14 Founding member of the Dada movement
18 Escaping movement, in ballet
20 Country music star who recently came out of retirement
22 Architect whose firm is designing the Nascar Hall of Fame
26 "Black Nativity" playwright
28 She sang "Paper Planes" at the 2009 Grammy Awards
29 "La ___ en Rose" (Piaf theme song)

Answers on Page 31

MUDEYUM

The Year in the Arts

CALADRIO

CALADRIO • Robu had to create an identity for an IT security audit firm and took inspiration from Japanese origami, which is both ancient and modern at the same time. **DESIGN FIRM:** Andrei Robu.com **ART DIRECTOR, DESIGNER, AND ILLUSTRATOR:** Andrei Robu **CLIENT:** Caladrio **PRIMARY FONT:** Futura

THE ABSOLUTE VIOLATION • The transformation of the headline into the tie that binds the victim's hand is the essential typographic metamorphosis in this image. **DESIGN FIRM:** Salamander Hill Design **DESIGNER:** David Drummond **CLIENT:** Susanne McAdam **PUBLISHER:** McGill-Queen's University Press **PRIMARY FONT:** Trade Gothic

[COOL CATS]

COOL CATS • The metamorphosis here is vivid as the two "Cs" in "Cool Cats" transmute into the face of a cool cat. **DESIGNER:** Ken DeLago **CLIENT:** Cool Cats **PRIMARY FONT:** Big Caslon

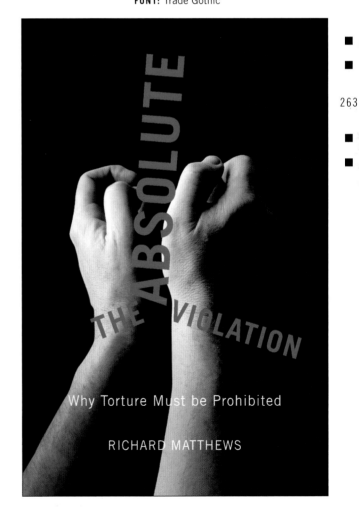

METAPHORICAL

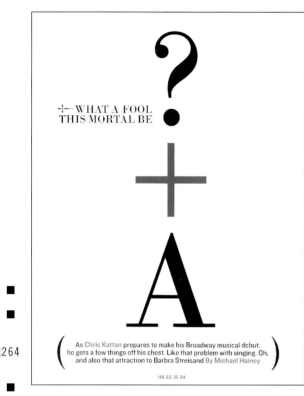

─┼─ WHAT A FOOL
THIS MORTAL BE

? + A

(As Chris Kattan prepares to make his Broadway musical debut, he gets a few things off his chest. Like that problem with singing. Oh, and also that attraction to Barbra Streisand By Michael Hainey)

166.GQ.3E.04

264

? + A • Is it just us, or does the headline look like a person? **DESIGN FIRM:** *GQ* **DESIGN DIRECTOR:** Fred Woodward **DESIGNER:** Ken DeLago **CLIENT:** Condé Nast **PRIMARY FONT:** Bodoni

DESOUZA BUSINESS CARD • The handle of this hammer, made up of Robson DeSouza's business information, is a perfect example of the modern visual pun **DESIGN FIRM:** Oliver Munday Group (OMG) **DESIGNER:** Oliver Munday **CLIENT:** Robson DeSouza **PRIMARY FONT:** Univers

ROBSON DE SOUZA ▶ ROBSON.DESOUZA@LIVE.COM
HOME *IMPROVEMENT* & *CUSTOM* CARPENTRY ▸ MOBILE 571 730 8940

TCM POSTERS • These promotions for Turner Classic Movies (TCM) transform boilerplate movie tickets into a typographic frame for the posters themselves. **DESIGN FIRM:** Wink **ART DIRECTORS:** Richard Boynton, Scott Thares **DESIGNER:** Richard Boynton **CLIENT:** Turner Classic Movies **PRIMARY FONTS:** Helvetica, Futura

FILM No. 000859 CK

ALL THIS MAN REALLY WANTS IS:
More money? More power? More fame? HIS CHILDHOOD?

THERE'S A REASON THEY'RE CALLED CLASSICS.

MOVIES

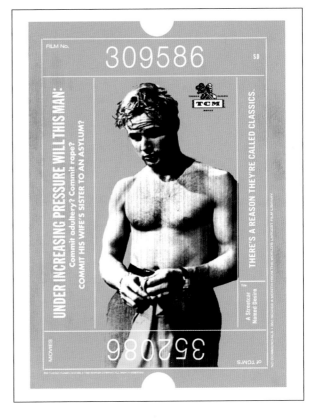

FILM No. 309586 SD

UNDER INCREASING PRESSURE WILL THIS MAN:
Commit adultery? Commit rape?
COMMIT HIS WIFE'S SISTER TO AN ASYLUM?

THERE'S A REASON THEY'RE CALLED CLASSICS.

MOVIES

METAPHORICAL

THE FATE OF THE NATION STATE • The type for this cover is imprisoned within a makeshift jail. **DESIGN FIRM:** Salamander Hill Design **DESIGNER:** David Drummond **CLIENT:** Susanne McAdam **PUBLISHER:** McGill-Queen's University Press **PRIMARY FONTS:** Trade Gothic, Grotesque

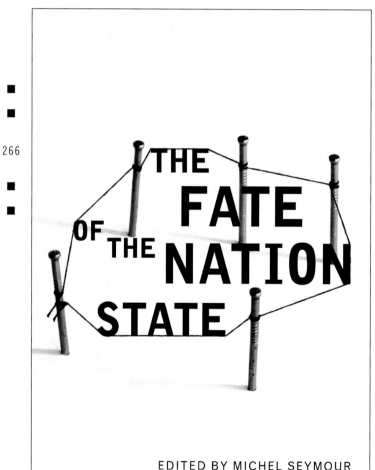

ELECTRIC COMPANY CONSULTING • Electric Company Consulting, an integrated marketing agency, was looking to update their graphic identity. The agency offers various tools, such as the "Power Panel," which taps into the power of some of the country's best creative thinkers. Wink encouraged them to choose a bold and simple graphic, one that would speak to the thinking and the energy of the company – hence the head as lightbulb. **DESIGN FIRM:** Wink **ART DIRECTORS:** Scott Thares, Richard Boynton **DESIGNER AND ILLUSTRATOR:** Scott Thares **CLIENT:** Electric Company Consulting **PRIMARY FONTS:** Helvetica, Futura

Françoise
Sagan

Bonjour
Tristesse

With a New Introduction by Diane Johnson

BONJOUR TRISTESSE • This is a book
jacket for a novel about a girl's coming of
age in the 1950s. It echoes Saul Bass's
movie poster for the Otto Preminger
film that was adapted from the same
book. **DESIGN FIRM:** HarperCollins **ART
DIRECTOR AND DESIGNER:** Roberto
de Vicq de Cumptich **CLIENT:** Ecco
PUBLISHER: HarperCollins **PRIMARY
FONT:** Helvetica Neue

METAPHORICAL

OIL, TIMBER, AND COLTAN • In these book cover designs oil, timber, and coltan are transformed into a frame for the message. **DESIGN FIRM:** Salamander Hill Design **DESIGNER:** David Drummond **CLIENT:** Neil de Cort **PUBLISHER:** Polity Press **PRIMARY FONTS:** Trade Gothic, Frutiger

PETER DAUVERGNE

PHILIPPE LE BILLON AND GAVIN BRIDGE

MICHAEL NEST

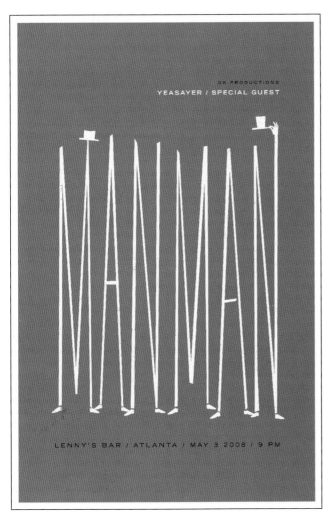

MAN MAN • An idiosyncratic type treatment featuring a personification of the band's name, this poster was created to advertise a concert in Atlanta. Diec and Moore were inspired by the playful, human quality of Man Man's music. **DESIGNERS:** Alvin Diec, Shelley Moore **CLIENT:** Man Man **PRIMARY FONTS:** Hand-drawn, Trade Gothic

LEED FOR HOMES REFERENCE GUIDE • The U.S. Green Building Council's LEED guidelines for green building are the most widely followed benchmarks for environmentally friendly constructions. "For this book cover," explains Willen, "we created a typographic house built with the benefits and advantages of a green home." **DESIGN FIRM:** Post Typography **ART DIRECTORS:** Nolen Strals, Bruce Willen **DESIGNER AND PHOTOGRAPHER:** Bruce Willen **CLIENT:** U.S. Green Building Council (USGBC) **PRIMARY FONT:** Trade Gothic

Baines, Phil and Catherine Dixon,
SIGNS: LETTERING IN THE ENVIRONMENT
(London: Laurence King, 2008)

Bataille, Marion,
ABC3D (New York: Roaring Brook
Press, 2008)

Blackwell, Lewis,
20TH CENTURY TYPE (New York:
Rizzoli, 1992)

Burke, Christopher,
**ACTIVE LITERATURE: JAN TSCHICHOLD AND
NEW TYPOGRAPHY** (London: Hyphen
Press, 2008)

Crimlis, Roger and Alwyn W. Turner,
CULT ROCK POSTERS (New York: Billboard
Books, 2006)

Eason, Ron and Sarah Rookledge,
**ROOKLEDGE'S INTERNATIONAL DIRECTORY
OF TYPE DESIGNERS** (New York:
The Sarabande Press, 1994)

Glaser, Milton,
GRAPHIC DESIGN (Woodstock:
The Overlook Press, 1973)

Glaser, Milton,
DRAWING IS THINKING (New York:
The Overlook Press, 2008)

Gordon, Bob (ed.),
**1000 FONTS: AN ILLUSTRATED GUIDE
TO FINDING THE RIGHT TYPEFACE** (San
Francisco: Chronicle Books, 2009)

Hayes, Clay,
**GIG POSTERS: ROCK SHOW ART OF THE
21ST CENTURY** (Philadelphia: Quirk,
2009)

Heller, Steven and Gail Anderson,
**NEW VINTAGE TYPE: CLASSIC FONTS FOR
THE DIGITAL AGE** (London and New York:
Thames & Hudson, 2007)

Heller, Steven and Mirko Ilić,
**HANDWRITTEN: EXPRESSIVE LETTERING IN
THE DIGITAL AGE** (London and New York:
Thames & Hudson, 2006)

Heller, Steven and Mirko Ilić,
**ANATOMY OF DESIGN: UNCOVERING THE
INFLUENCES AND INSPIRATION IN MODERN
GRAPHIC DESIGN** (Beverly: Rockport
Publishers, 2007)

Heller, Steven and Louise Fili,
**DESIGN CONNOISSEUR; AN ECLECTIC
COLLECTION OF IMAGERY AND TYPE**
(New York: Allworth Press, 2000)

Heller, Steven and Louise Fili,
**STYLEPEDIA: A GUIDE TO GRAPHIC DESIGN
MANNERISMS, QUIRKS, AND CONCEITS**
(San Francisco: Chronicle Books, 2006)

Jaspert, W. Pincus, W. Turner Berry and
A.F. Johnson,
ENCYCLOPEDIA OF TYPE FACES (London:
Blandford Press, 1953)

Kelly, Rob Roy,
**AMERICAN WOOD TYPE 1828–1900: NOTES
ON THE EVOLUTION OF DECORATED AND
LARGE TYPES** (New York: Da Capo Press,
Inc., 1969)

Klanten, Robert and Hendrick Hellige,
**PLAYFUL TYPE: EPHEMERAL LETTERING AND
ILLUSTRATIVE FONTS** (Berlin: Die Gestalten
Verlag, 2008)

Lewis, John,
**PRINTED EPHEMERA: THE CHANGING USES
OF TYPE AND LETTERFORMS IN ENGLISH
AND AMERICAN PRINTING** (Woodbridge,
UK: The Antique Collectors Club, 1990)

McKnight-Trontz, Alex Steinweiss and
Jennifer Steinweiss,
**FOR THE RECORD: THE LIFE AND WORK OF
ALEX STEINWEISS** (New York: Princeton
Architectural Press, 2000)

McLean, Ruari
JAN TSCHICHOLD: TYPOGRAPHER (London:
Lund Humphries, 1975)

Meggs, Philip B.,
A HISTORY OF GRAPHIC DESIGN (Hoboken:
John Wiley and Sons, 1998)

Müller, Lars and Victor Malsy,
HELVETICA FOREVER: STORY OF A TYPEFACE
(Zürich: Lars Müller Publishers, 2007)

Perry, Michael,
**OVER & OVER: A CATALOG OF HAND-
DRAWN PATTERNS** (New York: Princeton
Architectural Press, 2008)

Poynor, Rick
TYPOGRAPHICA (New York: Princeton
Architectural Press, 2002)

Purvis, Alston W.,
H.N. WERKMAN (New Haven: Yale
University Press, 2004)

Rothenstein, Julian and Mel Gooding,
ABZ: MORE ALPHABETS AND OTHER SIGNS
(San Francisco: Chronicle Books, 2003)

Sagmeister, Stefan,
THINGS I HAVE LEARNED IN MY LIFE SO FAR
(New York: Abrams, 2008)

Spencer, Herbert,
PIONEERS OF MODERN TYPOGRAPHY (New
York: Hastings House, 1969)

Spencer, Herbert (ed.),
THE LIBERATED PAGE (San Francisco:
Bedford Press, 1987)

Tholenaar, Jan, Cees W. de Jong and Alston
W. Purvis,
**TYPE: A VISUAL HISTORY OF TYPEFACES AND
GRAPHIC STYLES, VOL. 1** (Los Angeles:
Taschen, 2009)

VanderLans, Rudy and Zuzana Licko,
**EMIGRE: GRAPHIC DESIGN INTO THE
DIGITAL REALM** (New York: Van Nostrand
Reinhold, 1993)

Vit, Armin and Bryony Gomez-Palacio,
**GRAPHIC DESIGN, REFERENCED: A VISUAL
GUIDE TO THE LANGUAGE, APPLICATIONS,
AND HISTORY OF GRAPHIC DESIGN** (Beverly:
Rockport Publishers, 2009)

Wozencroft, Jon and Neville Brody,
THE GRAPHIC LANGUAGE OF NEVILLE BRODY
(London: Thames & Hudson, 1988)

271